50 THINGS ABOUT A MODERN OIL TANKER

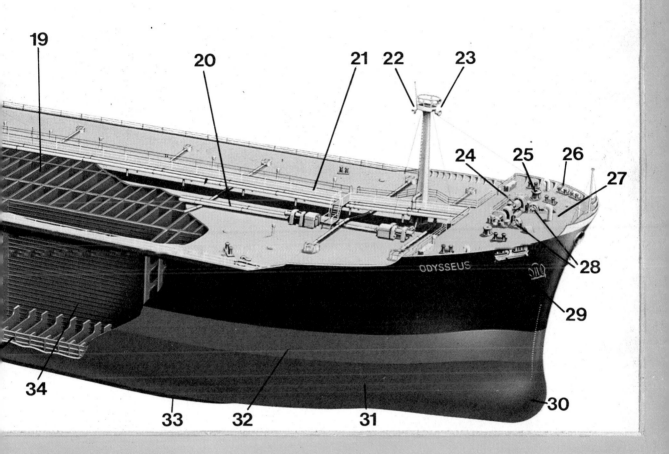

ODYSSEUS

down in the fo'c'sle is the chain locker for the anchor chain.

28 Chain stopper, this locks the anchor chain when the anchor is dropped and sufficient chain has been paid out.

29 Roller fair leads, the mooring lines run over the leads.

30 Bulbous bow under water which improves the ship's performance.

31 Position of forward pump room.

32 Position of cofferdam; this is created by two watertight fire-proof bulkheads with a wide air space between them. The cofferdam separates the bow section from the tank space.

33 Bilge keel.

34 Starboard wing tanks.

35 Stringers.

36 Heating panels. All tanks are steam-heated to thin the oil ready for pump-

ing ashore; this is done as the ship nears port.

37 "Isherwood" construction; the tanks are stiffened with closely spaced perforated bulkheads.

38 Tank inspection hatches.

39 Deck winch.

40 Fuel space for refined diesel oil for ship's engines.

41 Auxiliary diesel engines driving generators. A ship requires as much electricity as a medium-sized town!

42 Main diesel engine.

43 Cylinder head.

44 Exhaust manifold.

45 Engineers' catwalk.

46 Propeller shaft.

47 Five-bladed propeller.

48 Balanced rudder.

49 Inflatable life raft.

50 Motor lifeboats.

Price

80p.

Contents

© IPC Magazines Ltd. 1973

Published by IPC Magazines Ltd., Fleetway House, Farringdon Street, London, England. Sole agents for Australia and New Zealand, Gordon & Gotch Ltd.; South Africa, Central News Agency Ltd.; Rhodesia and Zambia, Kingstons Ltd. Printed in England by W. S. Cowell Limited, Ipswich.

JAPAN TODAY

No other country in the world is so overcrowded as modern Japan. That is the visitor's first impression – and he is so right. Yet, once outside the teeming cities, the pleasant countryside abounds, quiet and sparsely populated as in many parts of Britain.

There, however, the similarity ceases. The entire Japanese population lives within sight of mountains – from Mt. Fuji to Mt. Aso and a whole range of lesser peaks. And it is this feature that has created the image we all know as the "typical Japanese scene". Paintings and pictures show snow-capped mountains in the distance or a nearby summit lording it over a neatly decorated garden.

Japan is many things to many people depending on where one goes, what one wants to do or see. It is a friendly land if, at times, a trifle aloof in dealings with obvious foreigners. It is also a place of terrific contrasts. The traditional exists side by side with youthful enthusiasm for "catching up with the West".

Unlike Commodore Perry who effectively opened a door to what had been a closed Japan in 1853, we can nowadays expect a warm welcome, a courtesy second to none and a nation with more historical

Komoku-ten, who is red, and Jikoku-ten, green, are the guardians of the Niten-mon Gate. Komoku-ten guards the western skies while Jikoku-ten keeps evils away from the eastern skies.

Typical of Japan's modern image, the Meishin Highway is a marvel of road-building ingenuity.

treasures per packed square foot than the Victoria & Albert Museum.

Let's take a three-week trip to the Land of the Rising Sun. Mind you, we can't hope to cover all the wonders this dumpling chain of islands in a Pacific stew has to offer. Nor can we even begin to realise what motivates the Japanese. The most we can anticipate is to get the "feel" and the "taste" for a return visit. A leisurely sojourn at a later date.

We land at Tokyo airport, and a taxi is waiting. By the time we reach the hotel we are wondering why the driver isn't a Grand Prix champion or in jail for breaking so many traffic laws. But then, all Tokyo cabbies are the same — possessed of remarkable skill and an utter disregard for the rules of the road as we know them. Thanks to his driving we have just about noticed Tokyo Tower, the monorail, the bay busy with ships, the vast complex of expressways cutting backwards and forwards through the city. Only

just, though. And when we came into the down-town warren of narrow streets what we saw most were the traffic jams.

Almost immediately we enter our hotel we are invited to take a bath. Being a nation addicted to personal cleanliness the Japanese mean no disrespect by this suggestion. The bath ritual in Japan is one associated with pleasure and it is not unusual for Mr. Suzuki (their Mr. Smith or Jones) to linger for hours on end in his tub. Unlike us, the Japanese soap themselves *outside* the bath, rinse off dirt and lather and only then do they climb into the sunken, tiled bath to soak in near-boiling water.

Glittering City

We don't eat in the hotel. Instead, we wander round the corner and, beneath a lantern, enter a bamboo-decor establishment that has remained like this since the Seven Samurai rode to fame. For the occasion we select *suki-yaki* – a dish our foreign palate can handle easily. And don't be afraid. Japanese cooking is excellent if a little strange at first.

After the meal we really see the glitter that is Tokyo at play. Neon signs flash and attract in every direction. The whole city seems ablaze with happy-go-lucky colours zooming into the nightglow sky. Shop windows tantalize with displays of the latest *made in Japan* transistorized marvels — tape-recorders, cameras, radios, colour TV.

Nearly everybody visiting Tokyo for the very first time has one name on his lips — The Ginza. We look at it but we are too caught up in the fantastic lights, the coffee rooms, the tea

houses, the restaurants and the cabaret shows to enter any particular one. It is an experience, nothing more. By now we have sore feet and the incessant din is driving us crazy. As in most large cities in Japan the noise is really deafening. Loudspeakers blare, cars honk, shops conjure up an assortment of discords as if to propel everybody on to their roof playgrounds where excited children add their shrieks to the overall racket.

Japan's Glory

Thankfully, the hotel bedroom is tranquil and the beds comfortable – two mattresses one on top of the other with warm *futons* (quilts) for covering. We go to sleep wondering what has happened to the ancient Japan of strutting *Samurai*, *Sumo* wrestlers, and *Noh* drama . . .

Morning, and after a typical Japanese breakfast we are set to explore. Most people regard the emperor's palace as the central starting point for any tour of Tokyo and we go there. While impressive, the palace isn't exactly what we expected. It has charm, and beauty. But so have a great many other imposing buildings. There is a wide moat which once was a continuous body of protective water. Nowadays this forms a series of smaller streams and ponds. Here and there, gatehouses like medieval castles poke holes in the gloomy grey walls facing us. It is not until we reach the *Ni-ju-bashi*, or place of the two bridges, that we see the main palace entrance. Ah, we say now – this is what we had in mind. All those willows and almost rural garden scenery. Yet, somehow, the setting is ruined by those noisy streets and soaring skyscrapers just a few hundred yards away.

Next stop – Asakusa, a bustling shopping centre within Tokyo's sprawling metropolis. We've de-

Modern archer in authentic 16th-century costume tries his skills at a tournament.

6

Above: Horyu-ji Temple, Nara. From here Japanese culture spread to embrace the island nation in its infancy.

Right: *Torii* gates represent a rooster's perch. They are always a sign of the Shinto religion. Legend tells us the rooster crowed, the sun goddess awoke and the world was flooded by light.

Below: Nijo Castle enclosure. Built by a military dictator to rival the emperor's opulence.

Below, right: Part of Nijo Castle's ornateness.

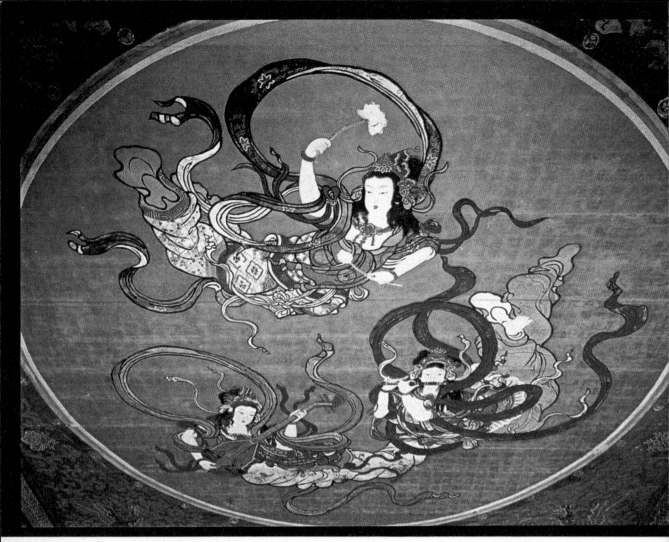

Painted by Kano Ryotaku the ceiling of the Sacred Palanquin House. Any slight clapping of hands under it causes strange sounds due to air vibrations.

liberately missed some supposedly attractive sights. And why not! We're here to see Japan's glory. Not just a collection of modern buildings and tourist *traps*.

Asakusa's magic lies in the bazaar-like atmosphere of its quaint alleys and covered passageways, gaudily decorated open-front shops and the irregularity of its block system. Time flies in those cross-hatched alleys. Articles of every description can be found and bought. Electronic instruments, fans, lanterns, foodstuffs, kimonos — even stuffed peacocks. Friendly merchants help us choose a few gifts — a *Samurai* sword, a wooden *kokeshi* doll, a beaded bag.

We are almost at the Asakusa *Tobu* railway station. Our luggage has been delivered and we are ready to depart on a privately-operated express train for Nikko, some two hours distant. We have reservations for the railway and another for a hotel, very necessary if we are to observe the Grand Festival of the Toshogu Shrine.

Holy Shrine

As we journey towards a most spectacular region we do our homework on the Toshogu Shrine. Built between 1634–36 it is the *spiritual* resting place of Tokugawa Ieyasu, a feudal ruler who united all Japan under a military-style government 400 years ago. So holy a shrine is it that until 1865 an imperial prince presided over the place. Even today, no one except the emperor may venture further into the shrine than the Offering Hall. Reading all the statistics concerning the number of artisans brought to the construction site, the fantastic amount of gold leaf used to gild the building (almost six acres) and the footage of wood used we are amazed. And terribly excited. Not only will we see this marvellous shrine but we shall also be present when the Sacred Bridge is opened to the public for the festival.

Entering the Nikko area is like a fleeting trip to paradise. Wild life abounds in this national park region, as do maple trees, cherry trees, silver birch, crytomeria trees and a wide variety of alpine flowers. Waterfalls and lakes vie with vermillion-coloured soil in pleasantly hilly country for honours. The town itself is crowded – nothing new to us now. All Japan is crowded. The homes are lath-and-plaster or wooden and, over all, is a feeling of uncaring. We don't mind. The real beauties are within shouting distance.

Sacred Bridge

Once safely checked into our hotel we venture forth to see the Sacred Bridge. Legend says that a priest named Shodo crossed the flooded Daiya river by using the backs of two snakes as a makeshift bridge. The cantilever construction does look like arched snakes with its far end vanishing into a clump of crytomeria.

We cross the river and enter the forest. Climbing slowly we pass the Rinnoji Temple and then – like something taken from the pages of an exotic storybook – we suddenly behold the Toshogu Shrine. For sheer extravagance the carvings, the precious metals worked through its façade and the vermillion colouring are almost unique. The mind boggles as the eye attempts to take in everything of beauty. Words cannot aptly describe the magnificence. Thankfully, our cameras record some of the marvels: the Sacred Palanquin House ceiling, Sacred Bridge, the Sacred Stable with the very original "Hear no evil, speak no evil, see no evil" monkeys. There is so much here that cannot be found elsewhere in Japan that the desire to linger consumes the artistic heart.

But, our time is limited and we must not miss the festival itself. So, regretfully, we retreat to the hotel and await the morrow eagerly.

Many a Hollywood wide-screen movie-maker would wilt at the scope of the Toshogu Shrine ritual. It is a cross between a Biblical epic and the home-coming of the winners of the World Cup! Three portable shrines in procession surrounded by more than a thousand marchers dressed in costumes of the 1600's. Samurai, soldiers, falconers. Others representing sacred lions, monkeys, fairies and four carried aloft by priests, supposedly the reincarnation of the sacred sleepers. We are lost in this ancient *Shinto* worship but we love the colour and excitement. Especially, we enjoy the dances and the archers on horseback displaying their skills.

Nikko behind us, we head for Kyoto the ancient and cultural capital of Japan. Our first sight of this very old community is a terrible shock until we realise that today must always co-exist side by side with the past. This is Japan's fifth city and an industrial complex traffic-jamming some 1,600,000 people within its

environs. But, again tucked into an hotel, we decide to see for ourselves what Kyoto has to offer. We walk – as all good sightseers should.

Within a few days our feet give out and the memory fades. There is so much to see in Kyoto that it would take a whole month to fully digest the sights. But we always remember Nijo Castle and the Fushimi-Inari Shrine.

Nijo Castle – not a castle by our standards. More a resplendent palace built by a military dictator to outdo even the emperor's opulence. It has a moat, turrets and a massive entrance gate but, essentially, this is a home. A place of exquisite craftsmanship designed to influence all who were invited to enter. Not a fortress to withstand an all-out attack.

A Nation's Heart

From the moment we enter through the enormous iron-plated East Gate we are in a wonderland of intricate wood carvings, murals, gilded ceilings. Here is the work, again, of Japanese artisans dedicated to their tasks. Painted sliding doors, spacious gardens magically capturing the contours of this island geography, profuse decorations recalling majestic sagas, legends, hopes for the future.

The same Shinto thought-line is followed at the Fushimi-Inari Shrine. Here the five dieties worshipped are those most important to the necessities of life itself – prosperity, planting, harvesting, coming of age and, not least, the fox who acts as the messenger for all.

Founded in 711, the Fushimi-Inari Shrine is one of the most

Japanese garden following natural contours. Fragrantly pleasing in its simplicity.

From the Toshogu Shrine's Sacred Stable the original "Hear no evil, speak no evil, see no evil" monkeys look down with patient wisdom on today's believers.

important in all Japan. "Pilgrims" carrying cameras – and Japan is a camera-conscious nation since they took over as a leading maker of this optical "toy" – flock to record celluloid worship as if a strip of colour transparencies had replaced some of the "natural" gods accorded Shinto "mastery".

We've managed to see other places considered a must by enthusiasts – Heian Jingu, Sanjusangendo and Kinkaku-ji. Each possessing special features and Treasure Houses yet, by now, not special enough to stay really fresh in the mind's-eye. Our time is fast slipping away, the pebbles of antiquity shifting under restless feet. And so we move on – to Nara . . .

According to Emperor Hirohito's family tree Japan came into being on February 11, 660 B.C., when an ancestor – Jimmu – was enthroned as the *first* ruler of "The Land of Great Peace". This happened near Nara and for many years the city had a supremacy unequalled (ex-

cept, perhaps, for Kyoto) anywhere in the country. Even today, Nara is the *sentimental* historic heart of this throbbing, vibrant nation.

Great Sun Buddha

Nine million tourists annually cannot be wrong – to borrow from another familiar saying about Frenchmen. The Nara Basin has much natural beauty, especially the park which thrusts like an arrowhead into the centre of town. Somehow this wooded, hilly, peaceful region brings back the past's magnificence in an atmosphere of regal cut-offness from today's bustle-hustle.

No visitor to Nara can fail to find the great complex of the five-storey Kofuku-ji pagoda. Thanks to the soldier-monks taking the wrong side in one of Japan's wasteful civil wars during the 11th and 12th centuries the entire 175 buildings were burned to the foundations. History's confusion walks with us as we marvel at the structures erected

here since then. And, especially, when we reach the Todai-ji – Nara's best known sight.

From the Nandaimon (South Great Gate) with its vermillion painted two-storeyed elegance to the *Daibutsu-den*, or the Great Buddha Hall, we are surrounded by pillars. Massive, soaring columns protected by guardian dieties and Chinese lions. But what is most striking of all is the immensity of the hall. This is the largest wooden structure in the world and measures some 187 feet in length, 161 feet high by 164 feet in width. Considering when it was built (1708) we've got to applaud those who carried out the feat.

And yet, we have not plumbed the depths of creativity. Inside the hall we come face to face with the Great Sun Buddha. What can we say as we stand in amazement and look upwards at this fantastic bronze statue – the world's largest again. Five years in the original casting this stupendous creation is all of 71 feet high and weighs over 550 *tons*!

Above: Nagoya Castle. Most Japanese castles were minor palaces never intended to withstand a siege.

Right: Ancient cryptomeria trees shroud the Sacred Bridge to remind us of the legendary priest Shodo who is said to have crossed the flooded river using arched serpents' backs for stepping stones.

Below: Shinjuku, Tokyo. Thriving community containing Komo Stadium which caters for symphonic concerts, ice extravaganzas and rock shows.

Below, right: Symbolic lantern. Paper variety exquisitely hand-painted.

It isn't until we have slept and taken a taxi to the Horyu-ji Temple outside Nara that we find another sight to excite us anew. Here is the cultural heart of Japan, the spearhead centre from which the Japanese peoples learned to accept Buddhism as an equal religion with their own Shintoism. Once more we have a five-storied pagoda with the upper floor being mathematically worked out so that it is precisely half the width of the bottom. The wood dates from 607 and it is claimed that one vault actually contains a bone of the Buddha.

Ancient Treasures

Impossible to take in, we wander and gaze on ancient treasures without honestly remembering each. Our three weeks is not long enough to capture everything with any great clarity. All we have done is get the taste for more exploration. We have not yet fathomed the Japanese character nor come to a conclusion regarding the strange ability of Nippon to cling solidly to the past whilst forging ahead with technological skill. We have managed to bring back impressions – the serenity of a garden, and the awesomeness of temples. And, overall, the tempo that makes Japan a tough competitor in a world geared to expansion, prosperity and an ever-rising standard of living. No two ways about it, Japan today cannot be denied her rightful place in the top lists of nations whose collective voice must be heard, and listened to everywhere.

Above: Toshogu Shrine procession during May 17–18. The *omikoshi* (portable shrines) are an integral part of crowd participation as they are carried through the streets of Nikko.

Left: One of the Japanese mythical creatures, perhaps a baby dragon.

Tokyo's *Ginza* is a glistening array of neons at night. One of the world's most famous streets: a serious rival to New York's Times Square and London's Leicester Square.

The voyage of the "Bounty"

When Captain Cook made his last long voyage of exploration among the Pacific Islands, the captain of one of his ships was William Bligh. Bligh was an ardent admirer of the brilliant Cook, and proved himself an equally good seaman, except for one thing.

Whereas Captain Cook was respected and liked by his men, Captain Bligh was not. His faults were an uncontrollable temper and a tendency toward unfair criticism of his officers and men.

During the voyage William Bligh learned a lot about the Pacific Islands. When he returned home, his experience made him an obvious choice for the command of the *Bounty*.

H.M.S. *Bounty* was a ship of about 220 tons, which was due to sail to Tahiti to pick up breadfruit trees. The plants were than to be carried to the colonies in the West Indies, where it was hoped that the fruits would be a valuable addition to the food supply.

The *Bounty*, with a crew of 45, including two gardeners to take charge of the plants, sailed from Spithead in December, 1787. They had a bad voyage out, and nearly a year passed before, in October 1788, they reached Tahiti. However, once the ship was anchored, all their troubles seemed to be over.

The natives of Tahiti were a charming people, simple, friendly and happy-go-lucky. They heaped presents upon the crew of the *Bounty*, who basked in the warm sun and enjoyed the hospitality of the islanders. The supplies of the *Bounty* were soon replenished, and the breadfruit plants loaded "in seven hundred and seventy-four pots, thirty-nine tubs and twenty-four boxes".

But so content were the ship's men on Tahiti that it was not until 4 April, 1789, that they finally set sail for the West Indies.

Perhaps it was the harshness of life at sea in contrast to the life of bliss on Tahiti that caused some of the crew, under the leadership of the master's mate, Fletcher Christian, to mutiny three weeks

Captain Bligh was hauled out of bed in the middle of the night and forced on deck in his shirt.

later. Or perhaps it was because Captain Bligh had been in one of his terrible tempers.

Bligh had openly accused Fletcher Christian of stealing coconuts, and had cursed his officers and crew alike. Fletcher Christian had born the brunt of his captain's temper for two weeks. He must have felt that he had suffered enough, and encouraged by the crew whose one idea was to return to their paradise on Tahiti, he overcame Captain Bligh while he slept.

The mutineers tied up Bligh and forced him into the longboat, with eighteen others who were loyal to him. Provisions, including 150 pounds of bread, 32 pounds of pork, six quarts of rum and 28 gallons of water, were thrown in along with clothes, cutlasses, a quadrant and a compass.

When it was suggested that a chart should also be provided, Fletcher Christian replied that it was not necessary. With a piece of paper and a pencil, he claimed, Bligh would find his way home from anywhere. Then the longboat was set adrift on the open sea.

The castaways rowed towards the island of Tofoa. Unfortunately, the natives there were not so friendly, and one man died. The remainder hastily rowed out to sea again.

Bligh and his men rationed their food to an ounce of bread and a quarter pint of water for each man daily. After a terrible journey of nearly 4,000 miles in the 23-foot-long open boat, they reached the East Indian island of Timor. Although they were well treated there, four of them did not recover from the hardship. The rest went eventually on to Batavia and from there back to England.

Fiery Fate

The story of the mutiny on the *Bounty* caused a sensation in England in 1790. A ship was sent to Tahiti at once to catch Fletcher Christian and his fellow mutineers.

It was soon discovered that much had happened since the *Bounty* had returned to Tahiti. Fletcher Christian had decided that to avoid British justice the mutineers could not stay on the island. The *Bounty* was therefore once again loaded with supplies, including cattle, pigs, chickens and goats. They set sail, carrying several Tahitian men and women with them.

The first colony that they tried to set up was unsuccessful, and the *Bounty* returned once again to Tahiti, where sixteen of the mutineers decided to stay. They were later taken prisoner by the crew of the English ship sent out to find them, and after many adventures the surviving ten returned to England. Six of these men were condemned to death for their part in the mutiny, although only three were hanged. Four were acquitted.

Fletcher Christian and his remaining crew left in the *Bounty* again to found another island colony. No one knows where it was. No trace of them was ever found and the search was eventually abandoned.

Nearly twenty years went by, and in England the mutiny on the *Bounty* was forgotten. Then, one

The "Bounty" made a long trip passing to the south of Australia and New Zealand before reaching Tahiti. After the mutiny the crew put Bligh in an open boat in which he sailed to Timor, shown by a fine dotted line. The mutineers sailed to Pitcairn Island, shown by a broken line.

day in 1808, an American schooner approached the supposedly uninhabited Pitcairn island. The Americans found a small colony of people who looked European, and, to their astonishment, spoke good English.

Although this information was passed on to England, it was not until 1814 that any more was heard of the little colony. Then two British ships anchored off Pitcairn island. Plantations could be seen from the ships, and people moving about. A canoe set off from the shore, paddled by a strikingly English-looking young man. To the amazement of

WILLIAM BLIGH

everyone on board, he introduced himself as Thursday October Christian, the son of Fletcher Christian!

The story he told was fascinating. Upon landing on Pitcairn Island, the mutineers had found water, wood, good soil and wild fruits. There were caves for shelter, and wild mountains where they could hide in case they were followed. They landed their animals, and took everything off the ship that they could possibly use.

The little colony had prospered. The mutineers had married Tahitian women, and had children, and they all lived happily together. Although Fletcher Christian and most of the others had died, one of the original mutineers still lived. This man, who had lived a violent and dangerous life, had repented. With the help of a Bible from the *Bounty*, he taught Christianity to his people.

As for the *Bounty*, when the mutineers had finished stripping her of everything they could carry, she was set on fire. When the flames died down, nothing was left of the ship whose name had become a household word through the mutiny of her crew.

SHOES for HORSES

Though most of us know what horseshoes are, nobody can say with absolute certainty where they originated. Probably the Arabs were the first people to use them. Certainly some form of horseshoe was in use in the East before they became known in Europe.

Until the 10th century A.D., Japanese horsemen fitted a kind of straw slipper over their horses' feet. Thick plaits of straw were carefully bound together and proved ideal for preventing the animals slipping on wet or muddy surfaces.

An early Arab horseshoe had six holes for nails, with a central hole. This closely resembles a type of shoe made in Britain which was called a "smuggler's shoe", shown top right. These shoes were said to leave prints indicating that the horse was going in the opposite direction.

Horseshoes were in use in Britain a long time before Caesar landed. The Romans never shod their horses, though the Britons continued to do so and gave the horses greater speed.

Horseshoes made with a turned-up piece of metal or clip in front are not recorded before the 19th century. The curious, clumsy example (right), weighing 41 ounces, is in the Guildhall Museum. These shoes were of advantage to heavy horses, though gradually lighter models with clips were used on smaller animals.

For the marshy parts of the country where horses tended to sink through the soft surface, special horseshoes were made. In the Fen district, large iron shoes which stretched well beyond the actual foot of the horse were used. These acted in much the same way as snowshoes do for people.

The patron saint of blacksmiths is St. Eloi, also known as St. Leger. Tradition says he was a blacksmith who lived in the 14th or 15th century. His skill is said to have been so great that even the fiercest horse stood quietly while the saint shod it. Plaques in the churches of Durweston, Dorset, and Freckenham, Norfolk, depict the legend.

Not only horses were shod. In olden days, cattle, geese and turkeys were walked to market and, especially before Christmas, had long distances to go from country villages to the big cities where they were sold. Leather shoes were made for the birds, while the cattle had iron shoes similar to those made for horses. An old carving on the stalls of Beverley Minster shows a goose being shod (left). Sheep were not normally fitted with shoes, but cattle were frequently equipped with some form of foot protection.

Today animals and birds reared for food are not shod. There are fewer smiths and their main business with animals is shoeing riding horses.

The Sweet Sound of Music

"What passion cannot Music raise and quell?"

Those words, written by John Dryden, the famous poet, are as apt today as they were three centuries ago.

But from the very beginning of history, man appears to have been developing the art of making music. Whether sung or chanted, or played on the numerous musical instruments that have been developed throughout time, it has enriched all societies, primitive and sophisticated.

The drum is said to be the oldest of musical instruments, in its most primitive form either being a hollow bough or a piece of hide stretched over a gourd or shell. Its ritual significance has been evident in all primitive cultures, arousing all kinds of emotions mostly religious or military.

In the times of the Parthians, about 250 B.C., drums were beaten to frighten their enemies, and warlike associations with the drum have persisted ever since. Today, in composer Benjamin Britten's "War Requiem", the effective use of drums creates an authentic battlefield atmosphere.

Of the wind instruments, the flute is believed to be the oldest. Originally made from bones, it has appeared in some form or other in places all over the world. Evidence has been unearthed of Sumerian shepherds playing to their flocks, and, in the pyramids, of a seated bard playing a double flute.

The bagpipe, usually associated with Scotland, is not actually of Scottish origin. The instrument was known in Ancient Greece, Egypt and Rome. Indeed, the Emperor Nero is known to have played the bagpipe.

By far the largest, loudest and most powerful of musical instruments is the organ. Until electricity was used, it was usually blown by hand or foot. An obelisk in Constantinople (now Istanbul) shows two youths standing on the bellows. And the enormous console in Winchester Cathedral took 70 men to blow it.

The harp is apparently derived from the hunting bow, whose tight string would produce a recognisable musical note. Modifications improved the tone; and fine examples of the development of early harps can be seen in ancient Egyptian tomb-paintings.

It is not too far a step from the early

"Drum beating" top right, in the most primitive jungle manner, while top left a Highland drummer shows the modern Military way.

Drums have always been of great influence in African communities. They are an essential part of most ritual rhythms, and may be used for communication.

The percussion instruments played in bands and orchestras today are a far cry from their early ancestors. Some drums can be tuned to definite notes by adjustment of taps, as in the timpani shown here.

Much of our certainty about early peoples' love of music comes from statues and paintings — as in this archaic terracotta (above left) found in Cyprus, and dated about 500–700 B.C.

The early Greeks were as partial to a musical evening as we are now. The sketch (above) is of a detail from a Greek vase or bowl, dated about the 5th Century B.C.

This Rumanian shepherd plays the pipe to his flocks, a custom almost as old as time itself. The pipe and flute are still played in their primitive forms.

harp to the psaltery, which could be said to be the earliest ancestor of the piano. The strings of the psaltery were plucked by the fingers, whereas those on the later dulcimer were struck by hammers. But with the invention of the harpsichord, the strings could at last be manipulated from a keyboard.

From these instruments came the pianoforte, customarily shortened nowadays to piano. With its invention, the whole range and tone of music was extended. In Victorian days, few homes were without their pianos.

The trumpet is another instrument steeped in antiquity. The earliest played only one note — according to Plutarch, like an ass's bray — but

The bagpipe was one of the earliest musical instruments in Europe, and was known in Asia. Though Samuel Pepys considered it made "mighty barbarous musick", its popularity has survived, particularly in Scotland, where there is a great wealth of tunes. At one time Highland pipers had to serve long apprenticeships to the instrument.

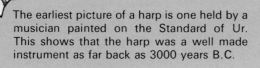

The earliest picture of a harp is one held by a musician painted on the Standard of Ur. This shows that the harp was a well made instrument as far back as 3000 years B.C.

The Ancient Egyptians enjoyed the music of the harp and not only did they show harpists on the wonderful wall paintings, they also made models of them which were left in tombs.

The modern form of harp evolved from many centuries of improvement on the original, simple, musical bow.

The earliest form of trumpet was probably an animal horn like the ram's horn or *shofar* shown below.

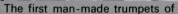

The first man-made trumpets of which there are examples are those which were found in the tomb of Tutankhamun.

It is doubtful if the Walls of Jericho could be blown down by modern trumpets shown on the right. The cacophony of the ancient instrument has now given way to almost any note within the musical compass.

Euphonium

refinements of the instrument throughout the ages have provided us today with trumpets that have a wide range of notes, many controlled by valves.

Associated mostly with military circumstance and pageantry, it is nevertheless an instrument that has found its place in more artistic music. From the trumpet, too, has grown a number of other "brass" instruments.

Perhaps William Shakespeare can best sum up the person for whom music does not hold some kind of appeal:

"The man that hath no music in himself, Nor is not mov'd with concord of sweet sounds, Is fit for treasons, stratagems and spoils."

The piano was invented by Bartolommeo Cristofori (1651–1731), a harpsichord maker from Padua. Many improvements have been made on the original, but all modern pianos still owe most of their essentials to Cristofori's invention.

Sometimes called the king of instruments, the pipe organ can be huge and complicated in structure. It can have up to five keyboards or manuals, a pedal keyboard and sometimes up to several hundred stops.

The figure seated at the organ on the right is an artist's impression of St. Cecilia, the Roman saint, virgin and martyr, who is the patron saint of music.

He saved sailors' lives

The circle with a line through it is the Plimsoll Mark for normal sea conditions. The scale beside it denotes the depth to which a ship may be loaded in different latitudes and different seasons.

UNTIL nearly a hundred years ago, there was no way of regulating how much cargo a ship could carry, and a vessel could be dangerously overloaded.

Dishonest ship-owners sometimes deliberately overloaded old, or unseaworthy ships. Then they saw that the ships were heavily insured. They knew it was quite likely that the ships would sink in a gale and then they could collect a handsome profit.

No sailor liked to serve on one of these ships. They were nick-named "coffin-ships", because the sailors knew they were quite likely to sink in bad weather, with the loss of most of the crew.

Finally a man named Samuel Plimsoll became very interested in the hardships and dangers which

sailors had to face. He went into the business of coffin ships very thoroughly.

In 1868, Plimsoll became a Member of Parliament and he worked hard, writing and making speeches, to get a law passed which would prevent the overloading of ships. There was great opposition from shipowners, who resented his interference, but finally, in 1876, he succeeded in getting a Bill passed. The Merchant Shipping Act made it compulsory for every ship to have a load line painted on its side. This is a line passing through a circle. It became known as the Plimsoll Mark, in honour of Samuel Plimsoll and no ship must be so heavily loaded with cargo that the mark sinks below the water.

THE BLACK DEATH

Ring a-ring a-roses,
A pocketful of posies.
Tishoo! Tishoo! We all fall down!

This simple children's song has a terribly grim meaning. It tells of the Plague, a dreadful disease that swept back and forth across Europe from the Middle Ages to the beginning of the 18th century.

The first line of the song refers to the red blotches that came on the skin as the first sign of the Plague. One of the useless attempts to ward off the awful illness, and even to cure it, was the carrying of posies of sweet smelling herbs. As the patient worsened, he began to sneeze. Then came purplish swellings on the back of the hands and under the armpits. These became sores. Very few people who caught the Plague got better and within two to four days they died.

In the month of May 1665, the dreaded Plague reached London. It held the city in its terrible grip throughout the hot dry summer and did not begin to disappear until the autumn. In that fearful year one Londoner in every five died of the Plague.

London in those days was very different to what it is now. The houses were very much smaller, darker and dirtier. There was no fresh running water and no drains. Rubbish and all sorts of waste was thrown into the narrow streets and every so often this would be raked up and carted away. In the meantime the streets stank.

Many people thought it was this awful smell that caused the Plague, so they tried to "sweeten the air" by putting cedar wood, bay leaves, lavender or juniper into pans of burning coals. All sorts of mixtures and potions were recommended for sniffing and carrying around on the handkerchief.

There were prayers said in churches (by the few clergy-

men who had not fled the city as had the king, his courtiers, the bankers and merchants and anyone else who could).

There were potions and charms. Some people even took to carrying dead toads under their shirts, but still the citizens of London died . . . at the rate of a thousand a day, sometimes more.

When a person died of Plague, the house in which he died was closed up. The doors were chained and the windows shuttered and nailed. No one was allowed in and no one was allowed out and food had to be bought and passed in by watchmen appointed to watch the house. Such houses were marked with a large scarlet cross on the door and the words "Lord Have Mercy Upon Us".

Inside the family watched and waited to see who would be the next one to sneeze and die.

Shops and businesses closed and few people ventured out and about. London took the look of a deserted city while grass grew in the untrodden streets.

The only traffic was the grim carts that rumbled by at night, laden with dead for the burial pits.

In 1665 nobody knew the cause of the Plague, but today we know that it is caused by a germ often found in the blood of the black rat, and Plague fleas that live on the black rat also bite humans.

In 1665 a bite from one infected flea was enough to kill a man!

In those days everyone had fleas and every house had its rats. People thought no more of them than we do of ants and birds in the garden.

As the Plague was ending the brown rat from Norway (the modern sewer rat) was arriving in vast numbers and it crowded out the Plague-ridden black rat.

Brown rats are a menace to health too, but they do not harbour the Plague flea, and of course cities are cleaner and healthier than they were three hundred years ago . . . and so are people.

ARTHUR, KING OF CHIVALRY

The Holy Grail.

"Whoso pulleth out this sword from this anvil is the true-born king of All Britain."

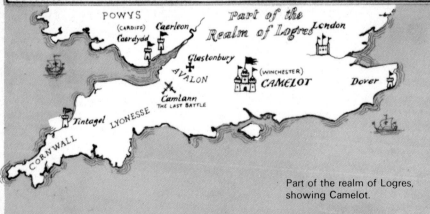

Part of the realm of Logres, showing Camelot.

POWYS
(CARDIFF) Caerleon
Caerdydd
Part of the Realm of Logres
London
Glastonbury
AVALON
(WINCHESTER)
CAMELOT
Dover
Camlann
THE LAST BATTLE
Tintagel LYONESSE
CORNWALL

Lancelot and Guinevere

Sir Tristram of Lyonesse.

Sir Mordred, nephew of Arthur.

Sir Galahad, the perfect knight and Sir Percival.

The Round Table.

Sir Bedivere throws the famous sword, Excalibur, into the lake.

Sir Gawaine and the Green Knight.

The barge of Queens comes to take Arthur to Avalon.

CAMELOT! There's a name to stir the imagination! A legendary city where King Arthur is said to have held his court. Several cities lay claim to the site of Camelot; among them is Winchester. But was Arthur a real person? Did he really have a beautiful queen Guinevere, and was he surrounded by brave knights? We do not know for sure whether there was a real King Arthur in Britain. Perhaps he led the Ancient Britons against the Saxons? Whatever the truth is, we still love to read stories about this fabulous man.

Merlin, the great magician, said that the future king of Britain would be revealed by a great feat of strength, and when young Arthur pulled a sword from the anvil, which no one else had been able to do, his prophecy was fulfilled. Arthur was crowned king shortly after this.

Do you remember how Arthur came to own the famous sword, Excalibur? Riding beside a lake one day with Merlin, he saw an arm, clothed in white silk, rise from the water. It was grasping a sword. At the same time, he noticed a maiden approaching over the water. She offered him the sword if he would promise to return it on his death. Arthur readily agreed to this as he was eager to possess such a fine weapon.

Many were the battles Arthur had to fight with his brave knights, and always his mighty sword swathed the way to victory. And many were the meetings at the Round Table, big enough to sit 100 men. The best knight of all was Sir Lancelot who was much loved by Arthur and his queen Guinevere. The quest for the Holy Grail is one of the most famous stories of the deeds of King Arthur's knights. But alas, bitter rivalry broke out between Arthur and Sir Lancelot. Two of King Arthur's nephews, Sir Mordred and Sir Gawaine plotted to kill Lancelot. They failed and finally Sir Mordred turned on King Arthur. They fought to the death. Arthur was carried to the place where he had promised to return the sword, Excalibur, and just before he died, commanded his knight, Sir Bedivere to cast the sword into the water.

THE MEN FROM THE NORTH

They were the first of the great sea rovers and they were known as the Vikings. An ancient Roman said of them that they were sea wolves that lived on the pillage of the world. And indeed they were some of the most savage pirates the world has ever known. The gleeful arrival on some alien shore of these bearded, battle-axe swinging giants bent on plunder, was inevitably followed by an orgy of murder and destruction.

Two things brought about the period we know as The Viking Age. To begin with, unlike the Mediterranean countries which possessed a fruitful soil and a balmy climate, the men of the North lived in a harsh, inhospitable land which led them to neglect the arts of agriculture in favour of a life of piracy on the sea. They spent their lives in planning and executing maritime expeditions. Fathers gave fleets to their sons, and bade them seek their fortune on the ocean highways. These ships, at first small – being mere barks propelled by twelve oars – came at last to be capable of carrying one hundred and twenty men. In addition they carried stones, great mounds of arrows, ropes with which to overturn small vessels, and grappling irons. It was ships such as these that began to attack England, Scotland and Ireland in the ninth century.

Eventually, the Vikings settled in many of the lands which they had harassed. They settled particularly in the little islands off Scotland – the Orkneys, the Shetlands and the Hebrides. They colonized Dublin and subdued great tracts of Ireland, and they also conquered parts of England. And this was still only a small part of their activities. The Viking, Rollo, forced the French king, Charles the Simple to give him a province afterwards called Normandy, or "north-man dwelling", while other Vikings were busily settling in Sicily. Constantinople was being threatened by the Vikings and others were raiding the coastal regions of Asia Minor.

The Vikings were undoubtedly cruel, even by the standards which operated in those early times. Their ravages were unstrained by any feelings of pity, and they seemed to suffer from a peculiar form of madness when they went into battle, which they themselves recognised and referred to as *bersejks-gangr,* or "berserk's way."

But there was another side to them which helped to bring about The Viking Age. They were, above all, a race of explorers with the same spirit of adventure that prompted men like Drake and Christopher Columbus to sail into strange waters in search of the unknown. Driven by this urge, the Northmen, without compass or quadrant, without any of the advantages of science, geographical knowledge or the support of any previous experience, crossed the broad Northern ocean and explored distant coastal shores, guided only by the stars and their own private resources of courage and endurance. It is for this they are remembered.

THE SINKING OF THE SHINANO
A true story of World War II

the November of 1944 the aircraft carrier
"Shinano" was almost completed in the
shipbuilding yards of Tokyo. It was a ship
of 64 thousand tons, and its deck was a 1,000
feet long and 133 feet wide.

The "Shinano" could carry 150 aircraft and her deck
was so wide that they could all take off together.

Gentlemen, with this ship, Japan
will be able to restart its
offensive in the Pacific. I therefore suggest
that . . .

Excellency! An extremely
urgent message for you!

What is it?

The General read the message and his face darkened.

Our Secret Service inform
us that the Americans are
preparing to undertake a
series of aerial raids over
Tokyo. It is essential that
we find a
place of
safety for
the
"Shinano"!

And so, on the 28th November, the great ship, on
which the builders were still working, prepared to
leave for a safer harbour. She departed, escorted
by four fighter aircraft.

The voyage will not be a long one. But keep
your eyes open! We may be within the
range of enemy
submarines!

We shall
be on
watch!

As it happened, it was on that very day, that the American
submarine "Archerfish" had reached the waters off Tokyo.
She was on a reconnaissance mission.

Let us go up and take a breath of fresh air. Surface !

Surface !

It was 17.18 hours when the "Archerfish" emerged from the depths of Tokyo Bay.

Let's just hope that no one spots us.

We're too far out for that.

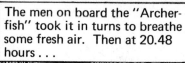

The men on board the "Archerfish" took it in turns to breathe some fresh air. Then at 20.48 hours . . .

Commander !

What is it

I'll be right with you !

Radar contact !

The Commander, Joe Enwright, went down into the submarine.

Look ! It is something big . . . and very fast.

Whatever it is we will tread on its heels. Get the men back down into the submarine. Start engines !

The "Archerfish" began to steam at 18 knots in the direction of the object, which the radar had picked up.

The target craft is advancing at 20 knots on a zig-zag course.

Calculate the basic route !

It is going too quickly for us !

ush the
gines —
hard !

We still
have him
on the
radar,
sir.

Good ! Now find out
if it is possible to get
anything more out of
those engines.

The "Archertish" was sailing now at a
speed of 19.5 knots — almost at her
maximum speed.

ittle
er . . .

Look ! I can see something
out there, Commander !

Where ?

t 11
clock !

Heavens
alive !
It's a —

It's an
normous aircraft
carrier !

Force the
engines
still further !

But the engines
will blow up !

Just do
what I
tell you !

mmander Joe Enwright sent a coded radio
essage to Supreme Command.

"I am following a huge aircraft carrier,
there are four fighter aircraft with her . . ."

An immediate reply was received from the Command in
Pearl Harbour . . .

Stay with
her, Joe ! We
are rooting
for you !

On board the "Shinano", work was continuing . . .

But the Commander was uneasy . . .

The fighters have not sighted anything, Commander !

Good ! But the voyage is not over yet !

On board the "Archerfish"...

The target object is changing route, Sir !

They're heading straight for us ! Submerge ! Take your combat positions !

Submerge ! To your combat positions !

Commander Enwright hurriedly re entered the submarine .

. . . which rapidly submerged.

The target object is approaching rapidly !

Up periscope !

The periscope rose up out of the dark waters . . .

In absolute silence the Commander looked through it.

It's an aircraft carrier, all right ! And here she comes !

...though still incomplete the "Shinano" was an impressive sight.

We are too directly beneath her. Hard to port!

Steer hard to port!

She's still coming on fast, Sir.

Hold it!

What is it?

There is a fighter aircraft right above us! Down periscope!

The periscope was brought down so that a fighter aircraft passed right over the "Archerfish" without realising that she was there.

It is gone. Up periscope!

There she is! She is coming this way! Stop engines!

Stop engines!

Ready to launch torpedoes.

A few minutes later. The "Shinano" had her side pointing towards the "Archerfish"...

And then . . .

Away one !
Away two !
Away three !

Three torpedoes streaked towards the great ship, three more followed . . .

Hit !

We did it ! Right on target !

Ship approaching !

Dive quickly !

The submarine dived as deep as she could go.

The carrier and her aircraft began a determined hunt for her with depth charges !

But the "Shinano", hit by six torpedos, was heeling over perilously . . .

And a few hours later she sank. Japan had received yet another terrible blow. The hope of her Navy, the tremendous "Shinano", sunk without ever having launched a single aircraft.

ARTISTS IN GLASS

Sand, soda, lime and colouring agents are the basic ingredients needed in the production of glass. Melted at extremely high temperatures, these materials fuse into an incandescent paste, ready to be transformed in a thousand ways.

The earliest examples of coloured glass which have been found to date are the ones which were discovered in Egyptian tombs dating from the second millenium B.C. From Egypt the technique of making glass spread throughout the whole Mediterranean basin. In the Etruscan tombs, for example, many glass objects have been found. In

Despite all the advanced machines which aid man in his work, true works of art are still made by hand. Take, for an instance, master glass-blowers who model one piece at a time and with great patience. From the "metal" (the sticky molten glass) gathered on the end of a long metal tube, the master glass-blower forms the object he wishes to make. Then, when it has cooled, he passes it to the grinder who finishes it, decorates it and polishes it. In the illustration above you can see some objects made from Bohemian crystal. These are true works of art made by master

glass-blowers in bygone ages: (1) A cup made in the Renaissance style, made in 1611; (2) A tankard with a lid in the Imperial style, made of engraved crystal and dated 1798; (3) A beautiful vase, dated 1840. At the top of the illustration you can see a

Bohemian, Maria Theresa style chandelier, with each glass drop worked by hand. By the way, the biggest chandelier to have been produced by a glassworks is made up of at least 9,446 drops, each one hand-blown.

Machines can make mass-produced bottles and cheap glass articles, but it requires craftsmen to create artistic glassware that will be admired for ever.

The modern glass industry revolves around the furnace in which the component materials are melted. These are the various stages of the process: (1) the store for the primary materials which will be used in the process (sand, soda, lime and colouring agents; (2) the crushing and the mixing of the primary materials; (3) the furnace which works continuously; (4) installation for the induction of the gas; (5) the making of objects by means of free blowing or by moulding; (6) a continuous belt for the lamination of panes of glass; (7) a machine which makes glass tubes; (8) the making of containers by the pressing system; (9) the furnace for tempering the objects which have been made; (10) the finished objects. The firing for the furnaces can be carried out by means of gas (as in the furnace illustrated) or by means of naptha, coal or electrical energy.

Rome, in the fourth century A.D. there was a street called _Vicus Vitrarius_, a street which housed the glass-blowers' workshops.

Throughout the ups and downs of history, glass continued to progress along its own path. In the twelfth century it reached Venice and then the little island of Murano where the master glass-blowers still produce objects in glass and crystal which are very much sought after, on account of the beauty of their shape and their wonderful decorations.

Glass provides artists with wonderful opportunities for beautiful designs for which great skill is required to produce the best results.

Two centuries later the domination of Venetian glass was broken by the Czechs, who produced the famous Bohemian crystal which is characterised by its brilliance and by the expert cutting which makes it seem like a precious stone.

Thus glass became used in works of art. It is light and shines brilliantly, and when it is ground for hours and hours by hand, and worked with great patience and effort, it assumes the most fascinating of shapes. It can be modelled into cups, glasses, chandeliers, bottles and table-wear. There was no noble house, no court in Europe or in the East which did not commission important articles of glass-wear from the Bohemian craftsmen. Museums vie amongst themselves for their masterpieces and today we can admire some of them in their showcases, side by side with those other fine examples of craftsmanship, ceramics and articles beaten out from gold.

The marvellous tear-drop chandeliers which hang from the ceilings of theatres, noble houses, and the last surviving courts in Europe, were almost all made by the Czechoslovakian master craftsmen. In their crystal drops, so pure and so very white, were reflected the breastplates of the dragoons, the uniforms of the hussars, the crinolines of the beautiful ladies when, to the languid sound of the waltz, Europe lived through a golden, carefree era.

The ancient Egyptians knew how to work glass into elegant as well as useful shapes. The illustration shows a head-rest, made from a block of glass which was engraved when the glass was cold. It carries an inscription giving the name and titles of Tutankhamen and was found in his tomb near Thebes.

A Bohemian engraving of the 15th century which shows us the stages in the working of glass in a workshop of those times. Today, it takes ten years to train a good cutter.

In the upper part of this illustration: Roman glass bottles dating from the 1st and 2nd centuries B.C. They were used to contain perfume and ointments. In the lower illustration, from the left: Bohemian crystal glass dating from about 1630. Next: a modern crystal vase made in Czechoslovakia. And finally: some modern wine glasses.

By day, the Blotched Genet sleeps in a hollow tree or stretched out along a branch in Central and South Africa. When night comes, it slinks through the undergrowth looking for small animals and birds. Two or three young genets are born in a litter at any time of the year.

BLOTCHED GENET

STONE CURLEW

The Stone Curlew, which is 16 inches long, comes to Britain in summer, living in open moorland and heath country. When disturbed, and running for cover with its head held low and well forward, its colouring makes it hard to see. At night, it hunts for insects, worms, frogs and sometimes mice. Two eggs are laid in a hollow in the ground in April or May.

EYES THAT SEE IN THE DARK

Many animals hunt for food after sunset. When the night seems as black as pitch to us, there is still enough light for them to see. You can tell why this is so by looking at the eyes of the cat on the right. Light passes through the black disc in the middle, called a pupil. When the light is dim, this opens wide to let in all the light it can; but it narrows to a slit to shield out any light that is too bright.

OWL MONKEY

TARSIER

After dark in South America, the Owl Monkey glides among the tree tops to find fruit and insects to eat, peering into the blackness with its enormous eyes. It uses its tail for balancing as it moves smoothly from branch to branch . . . the only monkey that hunts by night. Tree frogs in the East Indies and the Philippines are in danger from the Tarsier, a tiny animal that enjoys almost anything from snails to small animals. As a frog hops the Tarsier springs, catching its dinner in mid-leap.

GREAT HORNED OWL

North America's Great Horned Owl is really big. It stands two to three feet high with a wing span of up to six feet. When hunting, it swoops silently upon its prey — a cat, skunk, snake or even a young deer. As it attacks, the first toe on each foot, which is hinged, swings back so that it has two talons back and front, giving it a pincer-like grip. Its eyes, set in front of the head, are protected by a transparent second eyelid.

The Beginning of the

What do you do when you have something to tell a friend who lives a long way away? You send a letter. When you have written the letter you put it in an envelope with a stamp on, and then drop it into the nearest post-box. In a day, or perhaps two days, your friend will be reading your letter.

But if you had lived four hundred years ago, or more, you would not have been able to do this. In those days the king was almost the only person who sent letters, and they were despatches, giving orders to ministers and officials in other parts of the kingdom.

There was no postal service such as we have today. But there was a kind of Postmaster General. He looked after the messengers who carried the king's letters, and was called the Master of the Posts. The very first Master of the Posts was appointed by King Henry the Eighth, over four hundred years ago, in 1509.

The postmen of those days were called runners or postboys, and they rode horses from place to place. They were not supposed to go faster than seven miles an hour, but they seldom managed to travel even at four miles an hour. You can imagine how long it took for letters to arrive at that speed.

If the weather was cold, the postboy often stopped at a wayside inn much longer than he was supposed to for food and a rest. Sometimes people sent private letters to their friends or families by the postboy. Some of them wrote on the back, "*Haste, post, haste,*" in the hope that the postboy would think it was urgent and ride faster.

A few people did try to run their own postal service, but this was stopped in the time of King Charles the First. Only those employed by the King's Postmaster General were allowed to carry letters. The penalty for robbing a postboy was death, but even so, it was quite a dangerous life, for in lonely places thieves were quite likely to be waiting to rob the postboy.

Below is an early Royal Mail co

In lonely places, thieves were quite likely to be waiting to rob the post-boy.

Postal Service

Each town on the postboy's route had a post-master of its own, to supply the postboys with fresh horses, and he was usually the inn-keeper.

When the stagecoaches started going to all parts of the country, it was easier to send letters. There were special mail coaches, which carried letters, parcels and newspapers. As they passed through the towns and villages, the coach drivers told people about important events that had happened.

The coachman had with him a mail guard, employed by the Post Office. He wore a bright uniform and carried a pistol to scare away highwaymen. It was not always an easy job. As the coach went fast over the rough roads, the guard was sometimes thrown off and left behind in the road without anyone realising it.

When the railways came, just over a hundred years ago, it made the sending of letters much easier and quicker, but it was still too costly for poor people to send letters. The person who received the letter had to pay for it, and the farther the letter had to travel the more it cost.

Then a man named Rowland Hill put forward a plan to charge one penny for every letter, no matter where it went. The sender had to pay, instead of the receiver.

Fortunately, with the introduction of the modern postal service, the sending and receiving of letters is a service everyone can enjoy.

Above you can see what the world's first postage stamp – the "Penny Black" – looked like.

Before stamps could be bought and stuck on envelopes, the receiver of a letter had to pay for it.

guard is throwing sacks of letters to a toll-gate keeper as the coach passes through.

Pioneers of the sky

Coming late in World War I, the American aircraft designers and manufacturers were denied the opportunity of making their mark in the field of fighter aircraft and bombers. What they did instead was valuable pioneer work in the 1920s and 1930s which was to lead to the multi-gun fighters and bombers of World War II.

In the early years between World Wars I and II the Americans like ourselves, made many fine aeroplanes for which the free world was to be thankful when Hitler's Nazi forces threatened to enslave mankind. The planes both countries produced could not be tested effectively under battle conditions, but they provided the necessary groundwork to build ultimately the fighters and bombers which were to play such a large part in winning World War II. In these pages we take a look at some of the American aircraft of this period. They are of particular interest, mainly because they were the products of a time when aeronautical designers were not governed by the necessity to design planes scheduled for mass production.

The Curtiss JN-4, which came into being in 1916, had a romantic career which lasted until 1927, when it was retired from service. Carefree American civilian pilots, travelling the country with air circuses, used it frequently, treating the nation to a thrill of a lifetime at a dollar a ride. Earlier, it had seen action in a passive sort of way when it was used as an observation plane during the Mexican "incident" of 1916, when General Pershing's men were chasing the notorious bandit, Pancho Villa. The plane was affectionately known as the "Jenny", and a number of them have been preserved in various museums in America.

The Breguet 14 was one of the famous American two-seater bombers of World War I. Produced in vast quantities, it served air forces around the world through the 1920's, and to some extent in the 1930's. A bewildering array of these ugly looking, but dependable biplanes assumed many forms, including, eventually, ambulances and enclosed cabin transports.

It was created by a famous French aero-engineer named Louis Breguet, who was one of the very first designers to apply flaps on the bottom wing's trailing-edges to reduce landing speed. For pilots it had the further advantage of having fuel tanks which had been armour-plated.

The Curtiss JN-4

38D29

Breguet 14

In the closing weeks of World War I, the gaily coloured Spads of the American Expeditionary Forces could be seen roaming the skies above the battlefields of Northern France. The famous American squadron commander, Captain Eddie Rickenbacher, and a number of other pilots used it to strafe enemy artillery positions, and for dog-fighting. With its scallop-edged wings and tail and pugnacious snub nose, it swiftly gained a reputation for being a terror of the skies. And with good reason. Mounted with two Vickers machine-guns, it was capable of aerobatics and steep dives which could make other types of fighting aircraft shed their wings.

After the end of the war, it saw service with the air forces of Belgium, Czechoslovakia, Poland and Japan.

On July 21st, 1921, a formation of planes approached a German ship, the *Ostfriesland*, and aimed seven newly developed 2,000-lb. bombs at the stationary target. Two went wide, four were near misses and one was a direct hit. Some twenty minutes later, the *Ostfriesland* had vanished beneath the surface. If the puzzled reader is trying to work out what American planes were doing bombing a German ship two years after the end of World War I, we should explain at once that the *Ostfriesland* was merely being used for target practice. Just over a year later an old American battleship, the *Alabama*, was used for the same purpose. In both cases the planes used were the Martin MB-2, a bomber that came into being in 1920. It was the effectiveness of this plane's performance as a bomber which helped the U.S. Navy's thinking towards aircraft carriers for the protection of its capital ships.

DH-4

The DH-4, or the Liberty Plane, as it was dubbed for propaganda purposes in the U.S.A. during World War I, did not have the best of reputations. Pilots complained that it was obsolete and that it had never been designed for the big American Liberty engine, which had been installed in it. Much more serious was the fact that between the cockpits was a pressure-operated main fuel tank, which was prone to explode or flare up under enemy fire. For this reason it was given the alarming nickname "The Flaming Coffin." The constant criticisms levelled against the plane by air crews led to the refined DH-4B, but none of them could be delivered to France before the war ended.

The DH-4B was used extensively after the war for the air mail service created by the U.S. Post Office Department. Among the many other roles this plane played, perhaps the most significant was that of air-to-air refuelling experiments which began as early as 1923.

Martin MB-2

MB-3A

Boeing PW-9

Boeing P-12E

MB-3A

It is perhaps strange that the first American pursuit biplane to enter large scale production, should be best remembered for its performances in air races. Stranger still, perhaps, is that it was designed by an Englishman named Benjamin Douglas. First though came the MB-3 which was conceived in 1918 and would have equipped A.E.F. squadrons in France had World War I dragged on into 1919. This wood and fabric two-bay biplane owed much to the successful French Spad XIII. Although it was not such an attractive looking plane, its speed was far more impressive. The first of the four prototype MB-3's which followed was flown in 1919, and later clocked 168 m.p.h., an unofficial record for service aircraft. But what really established this plane in official quarters was its second placing in the much publicised Pulitzer Trophy Race, which was held in 1920. On this occasion it averaged 148 m.p.h.

Boeing PW-9

In 1922, the engineers of the Boeing company began to think of creating a pursuit plane with a stronger airframe that would be capable of absorbing the increasing power and weight of the new aero-engines. Scouring Europe for new techniques without success, they returned to the famous German Fokker D.VII fighting scout of 1918. With this plane, Tony Fokker, the Dutchman, had evolved a rugged semi-cantilever all-wood wing and an easily maintained welded steel tubing fuselage construction. Taking this plane as their starting point, they gradually evolved the Boeing PW-9, which was installed with a water-cooled engine. The plane, however, had one disadvantage. Although more manoeuvrable than its rival, the Curtiss Hawk, the PW-9 had a bulky nose which restricted forward viewing when taxiing along the runway. On the other hand, its tapered wings added greatly to its flying efficiency, and it remained a popular plane for more than a decade. Unlike so many planes of this period, no examples exist in any museums.

Curtiss P-6E

Boeing P-12E

In the early 1930's, the Boeing P-12E seemed to be the ultimate in biplanes. Certainly, it had superb flying characteristics. It was one of the very first pursuit planes to use a jettisonable belly tank which doubled its internal capacity which meant that this could be replaced by two M-3 bombs, which were additional to its underwing stores. The pronounced "turtleback" to the pilot's head-rest was dubbed the "Panama Kit," since it was developed to contain a life-raft for P-12E's operating in the Canal Zone. For operation in snow, which made it especially useful for Army manoeuvres in Alaska, the P-12E could even carry temporary skis which were fitted over the main wheels. A further development was the replacement of its traditional tailskid with a "modern" tailwheel, an essential modification when the Army Air Fields changed from grass to concrete runways in the 1930's.

Curtiss P-6E

As with its rival, the Boeing P-12, the P-6E traced its beginnings back to the early 1920's, at a time when the Curtiss Company had already built up a strong reputation for military-inspired racers. The P-6E was a single pursuit plane, the first American one to reach a speed of 200 m.p.h. It had a range of 575 miles, and could fly at a height of 27,400 ft. It was armed with two machine-guns, and could carry two 122-lb. bombs as well as light bombs under its wings on racks. Its reputation was made in the 1922 Pulitzer Trophy Race, in which it secured first and second places. From this plane, others evolved until it reached its ultimate with the shapely supercharged XP-23 of 1932, which achieved a speed of 220 m.p.h. But sadly, it was already obsolete. The age of the monoplane had arrived.

The End of an Era

The Boeing P-12B was first flown on May 12th, 1930, and 90 of them were delivered to the U.S. Army Corps in the summer of 1930. The P-12's rival was the Curtiss Hawk series, a more than worthy adversary. Both represented the zenith of the American biplanes, as did the Keystone B-6A, shown below, in the realm of twin-engined light bombers. But the day of the biplane was at an end. The ever increasing power of engines had left the lightly loaded wings of the biplane far behind, and the future was now with the faster monoplane with its heavy wing loading. Before we leave the biplane, let us take a last nostalgic look at the Keystone B-6A.

Boeing P-12B

In itself, there was nothing really outstanding in the Keystone B-6A. Its construction was certainly conventional enough – welded steel tube and fabric covering – but it was a reliable low cost aircraft which had been produced at a time when the Bombardment Groups of the American Army were on restricted budgets. It was therefore not considered seriously as a potential bomber plane, and was therefore put to other uses, such as bringing relief when natural disasters such as floods hit various areas of America. Potentially though, it was a good light bomber biplane that could carry an internal bomb load up to 2,500 lb., and had a normal flying range of 365 miles.

Keystone B-6A

Martin B-10B

Winner of the coveted Collier Trophy – U.S. aviation's highest award – in 1932, the design of the Martin B-10 was indeed significant since it proved to be about 100 m.p.h. faster than current service bombers and had the superiority over most interceptors as well. Taking full advantage of the latest aerodynamic designs and all-metal construction techniques, its inventor devised a plump but streamlined beauty with internal bomb stowage and semi-retractable undercarriage. It had a range of 1,400 miles and could carry two 1,100-lb. bombs. In many ways it was the bomb designer's dream come true. It survived long enough to play an important part in the Philippines during World War II.

Boeing P-26A

In engineering terms the Boeing P-26A was a half-way house, heralding the end of the long and glorious era of the American pursuit biplane, but just too early for the military chiefs to accept the departure of the wire-braced wing and the advantages of the fully retractable main undercarriage and enclosed cockpit. The P-26A was to be the swansong of the pursuit biplane because just around the corner was the B17 Flying Fortress. What Boeing produced in fact was a plane whose lines are exciting to behold even in the 1970's. Few pursuit planes of the period could boast the exceptional all-round view it afforded the pilot. Its maximum speed was 235 m.p.h., and its normal flying range was 635 miles.

Because of its headrest which had been specially constructed to give protection for the pilot in a bad landing, it had a distinctive hunchback appearance, which led to it being nicknamed somewhat unromantically, "The Hunchback from Seattle."

CAKES AND SWEETS

Fancy cakes and pastries were the fore-runners of sweets. The Ancient Egyptians made a variety of sweet cakes shaped like animals, flowers, fruit and musical instruments, and flavoured them with sesame and berries. These were eaten on feast days.

By the 2nd century B.C., the Greeks were making more than 70 different kinds of confectionery which were sweetened with honey. Shops and street-traders sold confectionery of many different shapes for festive occasions.

The Romans flavoured their cakes with cheese, egg, must, aniseed and caraway seed, as well as honey. Elaborate models decorated with figures and glazed with colour were made for emperors' courts and rich men's tables.

After sugar suitable for baking was developed in the 4th century A.D., sweet-meats were made in the monasteries. By the 17th century, Antonin Careme, a Parisian, was making sugar models of historic buildings and famous pictures.

"Liquorice Allsorts" were born when a sales-man for a firm making liquorice sweets called on a shopkeeper in the 18th century. The sales-man tripped and spilt his tray of sweets. "A mixture of all sorts like that should sell very well," said the shopkeeper.

In the 19th century, John Mackintosh met a girl assistant who was selling home-made toffee. He and the girl, whom he married, opened their own shop, sold their home-made toffee and eventually opened a factory.

Joseph Fry, a doctor who introduced cocoa-drinking to Bristol, founded a firm that became famous for its chocolate. When John Cadbury began making chocolate in Birmingham, his shop was the first to have plate-glass windows.

Sweet manufacturers were always search-ing for new recipes, and the search con-tinues today. One firm sent an expert on a 5,000-mile journey through the towns and villages of North Africa to hunt for recipes for unusual Arabic sweetmeats.

Today, the output of sweets is so great that machinery is essential. One machine cuts more than 4,000 caramels a minute, and another coats 15 tons of sweets with sugar in a week. Sweets are cooked, moulded and wrapped by machine.

The Changing Face of Britain

Wide, paved roads were built to carry troops and military supplies, but after the Romans left, the roads were neglected. The Saxons and later the Vikings lacked skill to repair them.

The roads of the Middle Ages were unfenced grass tracks. From autumn to spring, some villages were islands in a sea of mud, unapproachable by wheeled traffic. By the 16th century, the roads were so deeply rutted that in spring they were ploughed by a special road plough kept at the parish church.

Huge areas were covered with trees. The Forest of Anderida was 80 miles wide and covered much of Kent and Sussex. Essex, Surrey, Hampshire and the midland clay areas were densely wooded. In Saxon, Norman and medieval times, wooded areas were gradually cleared to make settlements.

The medieval kings declared many forest areas royal preserves for hunting deer and boar. Wolves roamed the forests. By Tudor times the forests were shrinking. Timber was felled for ship-building and to make charcoal for smelting iron, manufacturing lead, glass and saltpetre and for boiling out salt.

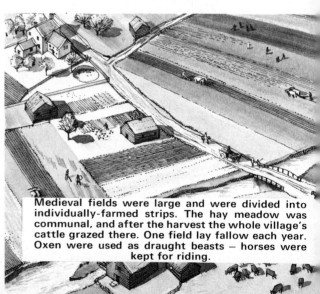

Medieval fields were large and were divided into individually-farmed strips. The hay meadow was communal, and after the harvest the whole village's cattle grazed there. One field lay fallow each year. Oxen were used as draught beasts – horses were kept for riding.

When the Black Death came in 1348–9, whole villages were wiped out and left deserted. The population of many counties was halved. Much ploughland was turned over to sheep grazing, and in the 14th and 15th centuries England's prosperity was based on wool. The Tudor Lords of the Manors began to enclose common land so that they could produce improved breeds of sheep.

Many river estuaries, the Somerset marshes (where early men built houses raised on stilts), Romney Marsh in Kent and the Fens (a huge area stretching from Lincoln to Cambridge and from Kings Lynn to Peterborough) were all undrained during this time. Roman engineers had built some sea walls and dykes, but these fell into disrepair when they left. These marshes were divided into river isles bearing coarse hay in summer, but which were mainly under water in winter.

The Fenmen were fishers and fowlers who paid their rent in eels. They made baskets from willows and cut reeds for thatching. They walked on stilts, used poles for vaulting from tuft to tuft in the marshes, and used boats on the rivers. In winter they used skates and sledges.

In the Middle Ages, most towns were walled and although the streets were narrow, most houses had gardens behind them. Villages were surrounded by palisades, or ditches crossed by gated bridges – not so much for military defence but so that they could be closed at night against robber bands.

The appearance of houses varied in different areas according to the kind of building material available locally. After the Reformation of the 16th century, few new churches were built, but many other buildings sprang up, often using the fabric of the old monastic buildings.

Much of Kent was forest in Roman and Norman times, but by Tudor times it had begun to be (as it is now) the "garden of England" with beautiful cherry and apple orchards and hop fields.

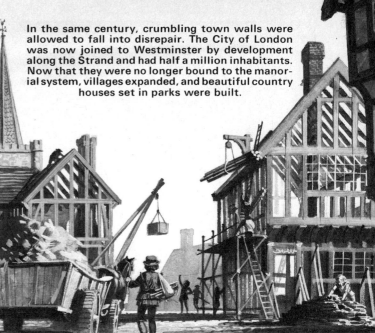

In the same century, crumbling town walls were allowed to fall into disrepair. The City of London was now joined to Westminster by development along the Strand and had half a million inhabitants. Now that they were no longer bound to the manorial system, villages expanded, and beautiful country houses set in parks were built.

In the 17th century, a start was made on draining the 13,000 square miles of Fenland. The Earl of Bedford, with Cornelius Vermuyden, a Dutch engineer, cut channels, dykes and ditches to drain the land. But as the water was drawn off, the land shrank and the cuts stood high above the land, so windmills were installed to pump the water. Soon crops were growing on land that had been waterlogged.

The Enclosure Acts of 1760–1820 did away with strip farming. Hedges round the new fields changed the look of the countryside and necessitated new roads which twisted and turned, following local boundaries. The result was our English lanes. There were farming improvements. Root vegetables were grown to feed cattle in winter and more pasture was ploughed to produce cereals for bread.

In the second half of the 18th century, the look of the North and Midlands changed radically. The coming of machines made cottage industries impracticable and factories were set up for the manufacture of cottons, woollens, pottery, iron and steel. Huddled round the factories were cramped dwellings for the workers, lacking ventilation and sanitation.

All the machines of the Industrial Revolution needed coal to drive them, so in the 18th and 19th centuries coal was mined on a larger scale than ever before. This changed the countryside by creating mining towns dominated by pit winding gear and huge slag heaps. Seaports such as Liverpool and Hull grew to carry the goods abroad and import raw materials.

In the 18th century manufactured goods were transported largely by water because the roads were still primitive. Rivers were dredged and deepened, but canals were the wonder of the age. The first complex connected Liverpool, Hull and Bristol. In 1792 freight sent by road from Liverpool to Birmingham which cost £5 would be only £1 10s. 0d. by canal.

was in this century that public attention at last ...ned to road improvement. Stretches of road ...re leased to Turnpike Trusts which undertook ...put them in order and, in return, collected tolls ...m road users. Metcalf, Telford and Macadam ...contributed to improved road making, Mac-...m's system of packing small stones on the ...face and then applying tar as waterproofing is still in use today.

The turnpike roads made "fast" travel by stage and mail coach possible although it was still arduous and expensive to take a long journey. In 1754 it took 12 days to travel from London to Edinburgh, but in 1776 a stage coach did the journey in 4 days (at a cost of 11½ guineas; in 1900 the train took 7½ hours and cost £2 17s. 6d.). It was suggested that, to keep the roads in good repair, stage coaches should be fitted with very wide wheels which would roll and flatten the surface as they went along!

By the beginning of the 19th century, England was becoming increasingly built upon. Factories, mines, mills and foundries were established in industrial areas, causing a shift of people from the south to the north. Men who had lived all their lives off the land were now moving from the country to the manufacturing towns. All over the Midlands and the North hung grimy clouds of smoke. The fields of the South carried heavy crops of grain to provide food.

It was in 1830 that the first passenger railway was opened. This proved so popular that in its first three months of operation, over 70,000 passengers were carried and over 4,000 tons of freight. The railway lines changed the countryside with their cuttings, embankments, tunnels and bridges, but quick, cheap travel altered it more as people moved about exchanging ideas. Big towns developed suburbs on their outskirts and dormitory towns about an hour's journey away sprang up when daily commuting by train became possible.

The railways took all the passenger business from the coaches, and much of the canals' freight. From the 1840s to the coming of the motorcar in the 1900s, the roads were little used except for local journeys. The motorcar opened the roads again, and wide, straight motorways have been built.

In 1846, a flood of cheap food came into the country from abroad and many farmers found it unprofitable to grow grain. By 1900, land under the plough fell by three million acres, but the 1914/18 war saw it cultivated again and in the 1939/45 war, even more was ploughed up. In this century, tractors have replaced horses.

In 1919, the Forestry Commission was set up to replant England with trees. So much timber had been felled in the 19th century and in the Great War that a shortage resulted. The soil of many places blows away if it is not protected by trees, and wood is still necessary.

With all these changes and developments, there is a danger that the natural beauty of our country will be lost. Much is done by the National Trust (founded in 1895) to preserve areas of great beauty, and a Town and Country Planning Act was passed after the last war as a check on unsightly developments.

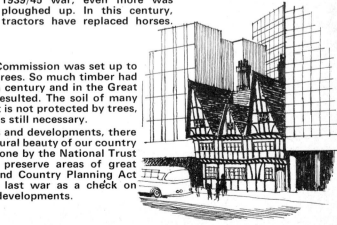

WHEN KINGS WERE BOUGHT AND SOLD

"Worth a king's ransom," we say, conjuring up mental pictures of coffers bursting with jewels and gold coins.

But just how much was a king's ransom?

Richard the Lionheart was captured on his way home from the Third Crusade in 1192 by Duke Leopold of Austria. The Austrian Emperor asked 150,000 marks for him (100,000 marks for the Imperial treasury, and 50,000 for the Duke). This was equivalent to about £2 million today.

As usual, the poor English taxpayer had to suffer. Enough money for a "down payment" for Richard's release was raised over two years by taxes on income and goods, augmented by fines from those who had supported Bad King John during his brother's absence. The balance was never paid in full, but the Emperor eventually let Richard go.

In the Middle Ages, ransom money – not to mention booty – was an important addition to a soldier's pay, which was meagre. A Welsh spearman, for instance, received 1p a day, while a mounted archer earned 2½p if he provided his own horse. Otherwise he got 1p.

So it was not only loyalty to King and country or his overlord that made the bowman or yeoman don his pot hat and leather jerkin and rally to the colours. There was also the hope that one day he might be lucky enough to capture an important person, who could be sold to his commanding officer, who in turn would dispose of him to the king (at a profit, of course). And there were "consolation prizes" as well, in the shape of humbler prisoners and loot.

Of course it depended on who captured whom. Many a gallant knight had subsequently to pay back a fortune he had obtained in ransom money to purchase his own freedom.

As in Richard's case, a king's ransom money was usually paid by instalments. The first payment secured freedom on parole, or in exchange for hostages, sometimes both, and details of further regular payments were agreed by treaty.

The ransom system had one great virtue; it saved many lives on the battlefield, particularly during mopping-up operations. No one wanted to destroy a potential source of income.

A good illustration is given by the 14th-century chronicler John Froissart. He records how, at the battle of Poitiers, the English knight Sir Thomas Berkeley was wounded and captured by a squire from Picardy, John de Helennes. After many politenesses and an exchange of names, John de Helennes wrenched his sword from the hapless Sir Thomas's body – the victim had been lying on the ground spitted like a chicken throughout the exchange of courtesies – gave him first aid and bore him to safety.

"Great Profit"

When Sir Thomas had recovered sufficiently to be moved again, his captor took him to his house in Picardy, "Where," says Froissart, "he remained more than a year before he was quite cured, though he continued lame; and when he departed, he paid for his ransom six thousand nobles, so that this squire became a knight by the great profit he got from the lord of Berkeley."

A noble being worth 33p, the great profit worked out at £2,000; less, of course, board, lodging and medical attention for 12 months.

During the same battle, King John of France himself was taken prisoner. The final price asked for was £500,000 (about £10 million today), but by that time he had changed hands several times. Although he had in fact surrendered his gauntlet to Sir Denys de St. Omer, he had been surrounded by a mob of men-at-arms squabbling as to who should have him. According to Froissart, the king tried to appease them by saying, "Gentlemen, gentlemen . . . do not make such a riot about my capture, for I am so great a lord that I can make you all rich."

The Black Prince settled it in the end, by paying Sir Denys 2,000 nobles (£666·67) for the royal prisoner, and then whisked the latter off to England where he sold him to his father Edward III for £20,000. This was a package deal, with another French nobleman thrown in!

Although it all sounds very mercenary, there was nothing grudging about the arrangements for the king's captivity; after a royal procession of welcome through the streets of London, he was installed in the palace of the Savoy, where he entertained freely. He and his entourage moved about the countryside, hunting, hawking and attending tournaments. There was a certain amount of excitement when it was thought that there was a

"Gentlemen . . . gentlemen," said the king, "do not make such a riot about my capture, for I am so great a lord that I can make you all rich."

plot on hand to rescue him, but he was merely confined to the Tower of London until it blew over.

After three and a half years of luxurious detention, the quarrels between England and France were sufficiently resolved to allow the French king to return to his war-devastated country. The financial terms included a down-payment on his ransom, plus an agreement that three of his sons be held hostage. The balance of the 600,000 crowns was to be paid in six annual instalments in London.

But while John was trying to raise this vast sum, one of the hostage-sons absconded, and the king felt honour-bound to return to England himself. He did so, and died there in 1364.

When King John first arrived in London, he was able to compare notes with another royal prisoner who by that time had "done" 11 years. David II of Scotland was taken in 1346 at the battle of Neville's Cross by John Copeland, a Northumberland squire. In addition to being promoted banneret (a superior kind of knight), Copeland was awarded £500 a year until he could find lands to the same value "as near your own house as you can choose them," plus a life pension of £100. This added up to an income of some £20,000 a year in present-day values – a fortune.

Negotiations regarding King David's ransom dragged out over the years until at last he was offered his freedom for 100,000 marks (£66,666·67), to be met in annual payments of 10,000 marks. The Scots sold the whole of their export wool stocks to raise the money and David went home in 1357.

Sometimes a prisoner not of royal birth proved a rich haul; one-eyed Sir Thomas Holland won a large reward by capturing the Count of Eu, who as Constable of France was a very important figure. At the other end of the financial scale was the poet Chaucer. As a young squire serving Prince Lionel, he once cost his master £16 in ransom money.

For sheer cheek, the exploits of the English archer John Dancaster take a lot of beating. Imprisoned in a French castle and too poor to pay his modest ransom, he escaped by means of a daring plot and, with a few English deserters, turned the tables on the French occupants, emptying the dungeons of his fellow countrymen. Then he ransomed the castle, lock, stock and barrel, to the highest bidder – who turned out to be the King of England.

Christmas literally means "Christ's Mass", and the word was in use in Anglo-Saxon times. Roman Britons celebrated Christmas after their conversion, decked their houses with evergreen and lit candles at Christmas.

In the Middle Ages, the poorest peasants enjoyed Christmas as a mid-winter break in their harsh lives. They lit bright fires, feasted and worshipped. It was a token of rebirth and that spring was coming. The earliest known English carol dates from the beginning of the 15th century.

In the Middle Ages, there were Christmas plays, feasts, singing and dancing in noblemen's halls, which were decorated with holly. In charge of the Christmas revels from around 1450 was a Lord of Misrule, who announced the Christmas feast, with its traditional boar's head. In Scotland he was called the Abbot of Unreason.

Priests used to open alms boxes on Christmas Day and distribute their contents to the poor on the following day, Boxing Day. Imitating this, apprentices used to go around on Boxing Day collecting money and small gifts from their masters' customers.

Queen Elizabeth I often spent Christmas at Whitehall enjoying entertainments, dancing and dazzling spectacles. Her people greatly enjoyed the Twelve Days of Christmas.

The holiday season officially ended on Plough Monday, the first Monday after Epiphany, when farm-workers returned to the fields. Schoolboys, working a ten-hour day, got the twelve days off. At Ludlow, leading Welshmen were entertained by the Queen's representative with banquets and displays, in return for paying their respects and giving him presents.

But by now the Puritans, who wanted simple religion and hated amusements, were menacing Christmas.

THE YEARS

In the 17th century, the Puritans tried to abolish Christmas altogether as a popular and religious festival. In 1642, they outlawed Christmas church services and festivities, and in 1644, they made Christmas Day a fast day! Naturally, people did their best to disobey. The Puritans threatened punishment. Town criers roamed the streets announcing Government edicts. Riots broke out in 1647 against these harshly repressive laws. In Oxford there was a "world of scull breakings": in Canterbury the mob broke all the mayor's windows "as well as his bones".

The Government stood firm. Christmas disappeared, except in a few homes. But when Charles II was restored in 1660, Christmas also was restored.

Now the emphasis was more on feasting than religion. A popular song welcomed Christmas, "Which brings us good cheer, minced pies and plum-porridge, Good ale and strong beer." Sir Roger de Coverly, a character created in the magazine called *The Spectator* by the writers Addison and Steele in 1711, kept open house at Christmas, and sent "a string of hogs-puddings, with a pack of cards, to every poor family in the parish".

Charles Dickens is often credited with "inventing" our modern Christmas in his *Pickwick Papers*, with its story of Christmas at Dingley Dell, and his *A Christmas Carol*, but he was mainly writing about what was already happening.

It was Prince Albert, Queen Victoria's German husband, who made the Christmas tree, a German tradition, popular in Britain. Christmas cards were started in the 1840s.

Until recently, Scotland, where Puritanism was strong, took far less notice of Christmas than the rest of Britain, but now the whole United Kingdom celebrates the great Festival.

THE INTERNATIONAL MORSE CODE

The international code below was compiled in 1851 from four other systems, which were based on the original code devised in 1837 by Samuel Morse in collaboration with Alfred Vail, his assistant.

A	·—	N	—·	1	·————
B	—···	O	———	2	··———
C	—·—·	P	·——·	3	···——
D	—··	Q	——·—	4	····—
E	·	R	·—·	5	·····
F	··—·	S	···	6	—····
G	——·	T	—	7	——···
H	····	U	··—	8	———··
I	··	V	···—	9	————·
J	·———	W	·——	0	—————
K	—·—	X	—··—		
L	·—··	Y	—·——	**Full stop**	
M	——	Z	——··		··—·—·

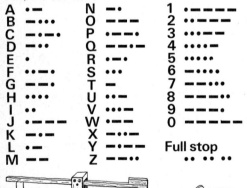

THE FIRST TELEGRAPH INSTRUMENT

The transmitting key of Morse's first telegraph machine made in 1835.

For thousands of years, people in Africa have sent messages to each other by beating loudly on special drums. The beating of the drums can be heard a long distance away and it has been called "bush telegraph".

Just over a hundred years ago a man named Samuel Morse invented a much better way of sending messages over much longer distances – he invented the electric telegraph. When Morse was born in 1791, electricity was just a novelty. It had no practical use. Morse decided to become a painter, but he was interested in science. When he left Yale university, he travelled around Europe, studying the works of the Old Masters and when he was returning to America from one of these trips, he began to discuss electricity and the experiments which were then being carried out with some of the other passengers.

Morse said he thought it possible to send messages by transmitting electric current through long lengths of wire and he set to work then and there on his new idea. In a few days he had rough drawings of his new telegraph to show the other passengers, but it took him another twelve years to perfect his invention and he was so poor that he had to make all the parts himself, as well as designing them.

DASHES

When it was finished his telegraph was a strange-looking device of clock-work, rolls of paper, a writing lever and an electro-magnet, but in the first tests in 1837, it worked. The American Congress agreed to a line being installed between Baltimore and Washington, but there was a lot of opposition. Some landowners refused to allow the telegraph poles to be put up on their land, others shot at the glass insulators and farmers used the telegraph wires for mending their fences. However, in 1844, messages were sent successfully between Baltimore and Washington.

For sending the messages, Morse had invented a special code, an alphabet with the letters represented by dots and dashes. A dot and a dash, for example, represented the letter A. It was called morse code after its inventor and today it is used all over the world. Morse messages can be sent in other ways besides the telegraph. Flags held in the hands can be used, a short movement representing a dot and a long movement representing a dash. Flashes of light can be used, or long and short blasts on a whistle. If you have learnt the morse code you can send messages yourself, just as easily as the people of Africa, over short distances. It is quite easy for instance, to have a secret message with a friend, even in a room full of people, by simply tapping out your message in morse on the arm of a chair.

Before you can do this, you will, of course, need to learn the morse code, and you will find this much easier than you might expect.

If you carry the code around in your pocket, and learn a few symbols each day, you will soon find that you have the complete code in your head and you may be able to read slow morse quite soon.

HOW THE MORSE CODE IS USED TODAY

Morse was the main means of transmitting messages for about a hundred years. It was used for telegraphing messages by wire, light, heliograph (a device for signalling by reflecting flashes of sunlight), flags and, towards the end, by radio.

With the introduction of speech transmissions (radio telephony), morse was only needed for telegrams and cables, and for long distance transmissions.

When teleprinters were invented, they made morse out of date because they use a different electrical code. Today, morse is used mainly for long distance ship to shore transmissions, where radio telephony is less effective.

SAMUEL MORSE

Samuel Morse was born in America on 27th April, 1791. He designed his first device for sending messages along a wire in 1832, and finally got it to work in 1836. The first telegraph line was opened in 1844 between Baltimore and Washington.

Amazement must have filled the watchers at the first demonstration of telegraphy. They heard a strange machine clicking away and saw a pen held by no human hand bobbing up and down as it busily jotted down a strange sequence of dots and dashes.

The marks the pen was making represented a message in the morse code. It was being recorded by the first receiving instrument invented by Samuel Morse. In this, current flowed through coils of wire wrapped round a bar of soft iron. This bar then became a magnet and attracted a metal bar on a lever, so adjusted that it struck with a click. When the current ceased to flow, the magnetic force was lost, and the lever was released and pulled by a spring.

As the circuit was rapidly closed and opened by the sending of the dots and dashes of the morse code, the lever snapped up and down, making clicks which were understood by the operator.

A pen was attached to the lever to mark the message on a strip of paper moved along by clockwork. But the pen was discarded when the operators learned to read the message by recognising the sequence of clicks. The sending instrument was simply a device for opening and closing the circuit, as does the modern morse key.

Morse used the canvas stretcher from a picture and some old clock wheels to make it.

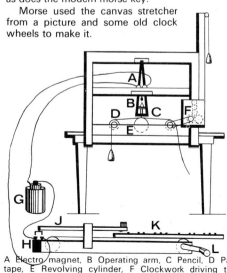

A Electro-magnet, B Operating arm, C Pencil, D Paper tape, E Revolving cylinder, F Clockwork driving tape, G Battery, H Cups of mercury, J Key, K Bar carrying message, L Message stick.

The Texas Rangers were formed in 1823, when Texas belonged to Mexico, by Stephen Austin the leader of the American settlers in Texas. Austin employed ten mounted fighting men to protect the settlers' homesteads from marauding Comanche Indians. This small band of courageous men became known as "Rangers".

In 1836 the American settlers revolted against their Mexican rulers. They went to war, won their independence and Texas became a republic. By that time the Ranger Force had grown and had been officially organized to deal with outlaws.

The Texas Rangers had no uniforms or military discipline and they chose their own leaders from members of the force. Their tasks included rounding up bandits, recovering thousands of head of stolen cattle, settling disputes, and breaking up riots.

Their reputation grew and outlaws came to fear the band of plain-clothes lawmen. But the Rangers' hardest task was trying to subdue the Comanches. These Indians were skilled horsemen trained to shoot their arrows when riding at a gallop after an enemy.

The Comanches invariably had the upper hand and they came to despise and mock the Rangers. The Texan's short-range, single shot rifles were too clumsy to be fired on horseback. Even their single shot pistols did not permit reloading before the Comanches rushed in for the kill.

Then in 1839 Samuel Colt invented the Colt "Texas Paterson." This revolver was a ·36 calibre, cap-and-ball percussion revolver which fired five shots without needing to be reloaded and could be used on horseback.

The Comanches had the shock of their lives when the Rangers opened fire with the new Colts. In one of the many skirmishes they had raced towards the Rangers totally unprepared for the withering fire that mowed them down with frightening speed.

Never again were the Rangers at the mercy of the Redskins. In 1845 Texas became one of the United States of America. War broke out soon afterwards with Mexico and the Rangers showed the United States Army how good they were at guerrilla fighting.

The Texas Rangers became one of the finest bodies of fighting men America has ever known. But after the Mexican war the United States Government decided, in 1846, that this undisciplined force should be disbanded and their duties taken over by the army.

RANGERS

The regular soldiers thought the Rangers had been a little too tough and the government decided that they could not let a band of undisciplined men take over a job which the army ought to handle. But the Comanche Indians and Mexican bandits did not fear the soldiers and the army had difficulty in keeping order.

The situation grew so bad that the people of Texas demanded the return of the Rangers — the only men who could successfully keep the hostile Indians and outlaws in check. So the Texas Rangers were recalled and reorganized.

Once they were back in service the Rangers acted in their old tradition of hunting down the enemy and hitting him hard. Toughness was the only thing that war-crazy Indians and hardened criminals understood.

Mexican badmen were a real menace because they terrorized the settlers and then fled back to Mexico. Frequently the Rangers crossed the border and made lightning raids after dark to capture these outlaws.

The outlaw with more Texas Rangers on his tail than any other was John Wesley Hardin. They tracked him down after he had been in hiding for three years. Twenty Rangers and three sheriffs, all heavily armed, escorted him from Austin.

Another outlaw who brought the Rangers out in full force was Sam Bass. He and his gang of esperadoes rode into Round Rock, Texas, to rob a bank. But someone informed on him and the Texas Rangers were waiting.

The Texas Rangers called their records of all wanted criminals their "Bible Two". At one time there were five thousand names on the wanted list.

Today the Texas Rangers are part of the Department of Public Safety of the State of Texas. They still protect life and property, apprehend criminals and assist in the enforcement of the law. The modern Ranger Force has patrol cars, motor launches and aircraft, but over rough country the horse still remains their faithful friend.

Folkestone Harbour was completed by the South Eastern Railway in 1842. Within a year, the first steamer was starting for Boulogne propelled by paddles and sails.

CROSSING THE CHANNEL

Today's cross-channel trippers have a choice of flying to the continent, going by fast luxury steamers, train and car ferries, or of making exciting, noisy dashes above the waves by hovercraft.

Their great-grandparents also had a choice, and they loved Channel trips. But how different were conditions in their day for their choice was between two rival railway systems.

Excursions to the Continent multiplied when the railways reached Dover and Folkestone. There were two rival rail systems: the South Eastern and the London, Chatham and Dover Railway. Competition between them was intense.

Folkestone Harbour was completed by the South Eastern Railway in 1842, and within a year the first steamer was sailing for Boulogne. Soon 100,000 passengers were making the trip yearly, among them Queen Victoria, who chose that route when on her way to the French Riviera.

Indeed, the picture became cut-throat. This was so intense that fares were reduced until they were uneconomical. Each company did its utmost to put the other out of business, and they almost succeeded.

When bankruptcy seemed inevitable, the com-panies were forced, by an Act of Parliament, to amalgamate and become the South Eastern and Chatham Railway.

This avoided the two railways closing down and saved the services for the public. But there was still competition for the sea crossing, as far as the standards of service were concerned.

An early advertisement of the South-Eastern and Chatham Railway tells of "Royal Mail Express Services via Dover–Calais and Folkestone–Boulogne." The sea passage to Calais took between 65 and 75 minutes; that to Boulogne from 80 to 100 minutes, with five services in each direction daily. "London and Paris in less than $7\frac{3}{4}$ hours" was the claim.

A picture painted by Howard Geach in about 1865 is entitled *The Boat Train, South Eastern Railway, Dover Harbour*. The engine, black, red and green, has a brassbound funnel. Coaches are "Wellington brown," with very pale salmon-pink upper panels. Waves are washing over the track as the train steams off the Admiralty Pier.

Alternatively, the passengers of those days could, if they liked, choose the London, Chatham and Dover Railway, running from Dover Harbour Station, to Victoria. A glimpse of this may be seen

Queen Victoria (above) chose the Folkestone to Boulogne route when on her way to the French Riviera. The Queen, with her ladies-in-waiting, is being welcomed aboard. Soon, 100,000 passengers a year were making the crossing.

A sea trip to the Continent was an exciting event. To go from London to Paris took nearly eight hours and the boat trains with their brassbound funnels (top right) were as picturesque as the ships of those days.

An attempt to defeat sea-sickness produced the Castalia (right) which had two half-hulls with a pair of paddle wheels, one behind the other, between them.

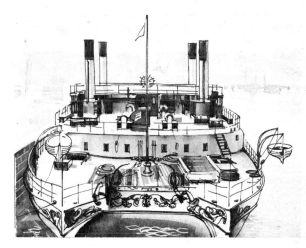

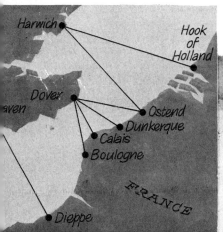

Every summer the steamers are crowded with holidaymakers and their cars. Car owners drive on to these ferries, and drive off at the destination.

As this map shows, Dover (and nearby Folkestone), Newhaven and Harwich are the main ports from which ships sail for France, Belgium and Holland.

in the background of the same painting.

In those days, boats approaching harbour signalled the numbers of passengers carried. Each of a number of balls on the foremast indicated 100 passengers; a ball on the mainmast meant 20; a flag on the foremast indicated 50, and one on the mainmast 25. A ball at the peak over the ensign, signified 10.

The early paddle-steamers were quite small – 300 tons gross, or less. Their speed was between 11 and 12 knots.

A day return-trip between Dover and Calais cost 15s. 6d., but many holidaymakers made a circular tour by way of Dover-Calais-Boulogne-Folkestone-Dover, which had to be completed within eight days.

"On a fine, calm day," says an old guide-book, "or when a favourable breeze enables a sail or two to be carried to steady the boat, the passage is full of enjoyment."

But who could guarantee a fine, calm day? Then, as now, the Channel could cause travellers plenty of discomfort, and designers were always trying out new ideas.

Attempts to defeat Channel sickness produced some strange vessels. One, the *Castalia*, was a sort of glorified catamaran. She had two half-hulls, with a pair of paddle wheels one behind the other between them. She also had four funnels, four bows and four rudders. Not surprisingly, she was not a good sea-boat, and had difficulty in making ten knots. She was soon dropped.

Another ambitious freak was the *Bessemer*. Double-ended, with four paddles and two funnels, this vessel was supposed to protect her passengers from sea sickness by accommodating them in a suspended saloon amidships. She rode heavy seas well on a trial run, then collided with a pier and smashed a paddle. She also damaged a pier on her maiden voyage. After a while, she was sold for scrap.

But nothing could discourage the travellers, whose numbers increased by day and by night. Charles Dickens gives a vivid picture of a night crossing in his *The Uncommercial Traveller*, describing the arrival of the night mail at Dover as follows:

"A screech, a bell, and two red eyes come gliding down the Admiralty Pier with a smoothness of motion rendered more smooth by the heaving of the boat. The sea makes noises against the pier as if several hippopotami were tapping at it."

In those days, words of command were constantly being shouted: "Stand by below!" "Half a turn ahead!" "Half speed!" "Port!" "Go on!", and so on. Dickens lists them faithfully; notes the "hiccuppy" South Foreland lights; the ever-present stench of oil; notes the progress of stewards examining tickets by the light of bulls-eye lanterns as they warn passengers that it is going to be "a rough night tonight."

Calais is reached at last, and passengers go their various ways, as they still do today.

Crossing the Channel on an ordinary ship takes over an hour. The modern Hovercraft cuts this time to less than half.

THE WORLD OF PLAYING CARDS

Have you ever heard of a King of Acorns, a Two of Bells, a Seven of Flowers, a Knight of Money, or a Three of Swords? Even if you have not, you will probably have guessed that these names apply to playing-cards.

Perhaps you had thought that everyone in the world used packs with suits of Hearts, Clubs, Diamonds and Spades, but you would be wrong. What we think of as English suits were really brought over from France about five hundred years ago.

Those people who study the history and design of playing-cards still refer to our well-known suits as 'French', although they are now used in all parts of the world in such international games as Bridge and Canasta.

Although French suits are used in most countries nowadays, the older national suit-signs are still found on the locally-used packs in such countries as Italy, Spain, Austria, Germany, Hungary, Czechoslovakia, Switzerland, and Poland.

Even those countries which use French suits have differently-designed court cards, which are mostly based on packs first used in France many centuries ago. Our own English design is based on a local Rouen pattern which has long ceased to be made in France.

At one time, most of the countries of Europe had, not only local varieties of packs of cards, but some which varied from one region to another within the countries themselves. In Britain we have never had more than one type of pattern. Cards first arrived here during the fifteenth century, usually brought back by soldiers who had been fighting in foreign wars.

Some packs came from places like Spain or Italy, but most were picked up by soldiers in France. The habit of card-playing soon caught

Some cards from different parts of the world: Top pair, *left:* a pictorial Ace of Hearts from a Belgian pack; and *right:* another card from a Belgian pack, in which each card shows a 'letter' from the deaf-and-dumb alphabet. Centre pair, *left:* a circular card from a Japanese pack, and *right:* a Knight (numbered 11) of the suit of Cups, from an Argentinian pack. Bottom pair, *left:* a Knight (numbered 11) of the suit of Money, from a Spanish pack, *right:* a circular card.

Top three cards are from a 1440 German 'hunting' pack, showing the Knight of 'Falcons', Six of 'Herons', and Six of 'Hounds'. Below are examples of the different types of suit-signs: Acorns (Germany), Leaves (Germany), Money (Italy), Spades (Switzerland), Acorns (Hungary), and Swords (Italy). German suits are used also in Austria and Hungary.

on in England, and soon, we were making our own.

Early packs were very crudely-made. The black outlines for the court cards were cut from wood blocks, and sheets were printed off on the hand printing presses of those days. The sheets were then pasted on to card, and stencils were cut to fit the various colours and suit-signs.

All the colours were then put on to the cards by various stencils, and when dry, the cards were cut up and made into packs. Only a very few of these early cards have lasted until the present day, and some of these can be seen in museums.

Old playing-cards are rare, because few people bothered to keep them after they had become worn with use, but some have been found, as part of old printers' waste sheets, in the board-bindings of old books.

Birth of the Joker

English playing-cards were taken to America by the early settlers, which is why playing-cards in the United States are very similar to our own. The Americans, however, made a number of improvements to cards, one of which was the adding of 'indices' to the corners of the cards. These are the small numbers, 2, 3, 4, and so on, up to ten, and A, K, Q, J.

The Americans were also the inventors of the Joker, which was originally called "The Best Bower". However, the English pack was not the first to arrive on the American continent. The Spanish had taken their cards to the New World earlier, and even today, certain tribes of Indians have been found using primitive 'cards' made of hide or bark, but with suit-markings similar to the Spanish ones.

Spanish suits consist of the emblems Swords, Money, Batons and Cups. Modern packs have indices like ours, except that they are numbered from 1 to 12, including the court cards. Spanish packs have no Queens. Instead, the courts are King, Knight and Knave (or Jack). Sometimes, however, the Knave is shown as a female, especially on packs used in former Spanish colonies, such as Argentina. In fact, the Argentinians have adapted the Spanish suits, so that Money and Cups now look like Suns (the Argentine national emblem), and Gourds.

A novelty pack made in England about thirty years ago, in which the cards have a black background, with the suit-signs showing as white outlines.

In Japan, early Portuguese travellers have left a legacy of Spanish-suited cards, which can still be seen in some rather strange cards still in use by local Japanese players.

Italy also uses the suits of Swords, Money, Batons and Cups, but in the northern part of the country, the design is quite different from that used on Spanish cards. In the south of Italy, cards are quite small, but the suit-signs are more like those of Spain. Depending on what part of Italy you visit, the local playing-card pack will vary in about ten different patterns.

Across the northern border of Italy is Switzerland, where yet another type of pack is in use. The Swiss have suit-signs of their own: Shields, Acorns, Bells and Flowers, used in a game called Jass.

Similar suits are found in Germany and the neighbouring countries. These are Hearts, Acorns, Bells and Leaves. As in Italy, there are several varieties of German cards, according to the part of Germany where the cards are on sale.

German and Swiss cards have no Queens. Instead, the court cards are King, Over-Knave (called the *Ober*) and Under-Knave (called the *Unter*). German packs are brightly-coloured and very attractive, and similar cards are also found in the nearby countries like Austria, Czechoslovakia, Hungary and Poland.

What is called the Hungarian pattern pack has a charming design, with all the Twos (or Deuces) showing scenes from the four seasons. Other court cards show people from traditional history, such as William Tell, Hermann Gessler, and so on.

Alongside the local-suited cards in the various countries, there are also some varieties of French-suited packs, some of which are very

These are the various suit-signs used on cards in different countries. Italian suits are found in Northern Italy, while Italo-Spanish ones are used mostly in the south of the country.

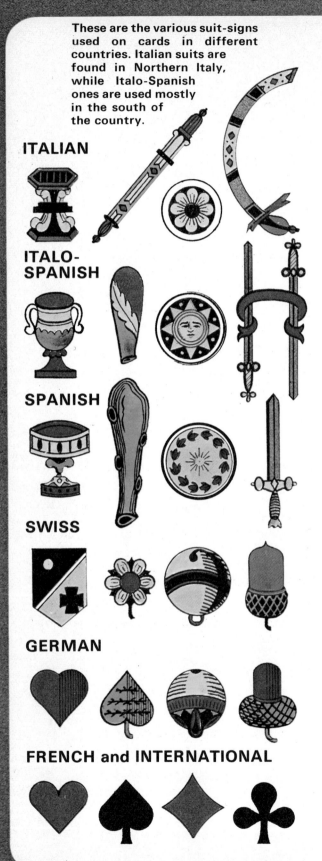

ITALIAN

ITALO-SPANISH

SPANISH

SWISS

GERMAN

FRENCH and INTERNATIONAL

bright and attractive. Nowadays, one can buy the familiar British-American packs in most countries, but there is nearly always some national variety which varies considerably from ours.

There is one type to be found in the countries of Scandinavia, another in Northern Germany, others in France, Portugal, Italy, Switzerland, Belgium and Holland. There are several individual packs of French-suited cards to be seen in Russia, but the indices will naturally be in Russian characters. Indeed, we cannot expect to see A, K, Q, J, etc. on cards from other countries, since the local languages use quite different words for the court cards.

In France, for instance, they are called As, Roi, Dame and Valet, and in Germany, As, König, Dame and Bube.

Cards of Fortune

In addition to the ordinary playing cards, there are other types called Tarot cards. These are often strange-looking, and much superstitious nonsense is talked about them, since some people use them for telling fortunes. In fact, Tarot cards were intended, and are still used for a special kind of card game.

The traditional Tarot pack contains 78 cards, and the usual suits are like the Italian ones: Swords, Money, Batons and Cups. However, each suit contains 14 cards; these are the number cards from Ace to 10, and *four* court cards, King, Queen, Knight and Knave. There are, in addition, 22 trump cards, on which appear various queer-looking pictures, with titles in French, Italian, or occasionally in English. Some of these pictures show such things as a man hanging upsidedown by his feet, a juggler, the Wheel of Fortune, a tower being struck by lightning, or the Devil.

No doubt these odd designs have led people to think that the cards had some strange meaning. They date back to the fourteenth century, and undoubtedly the designs have suffered from being badly-drawn at various times.

Many people have wondered who invented playing-cards, or where they came from. We do not know this for sure, although some people say they were brought to Europe first by the Gipsies. This is not very likely, as cards were known on the continent some time before any

Cards from Tarot packs: Top row: the first two are from a French-suited Hungarian pack; *right* is a trump 'The Wheel of Fortune' from an old-style French Tarot; Centre row: three courts from an Italian Tarot; and *right*, a King of Batons from a Swiss pack. Bottom *left*, is a Six of Swords from the Swiss pack, and *right* is a trump from a French Tarot pack.

Gipsies set foot here. Other people think that our cards were copied from the Chinese.

It is true that the Chinese had cards long before Europe, but the Oriental packs, which are still used by the Chinese, are quite unlike any known here. They are long and narrow, sometimes only three-quarters of an inch wide, and the designs are not like the European types. In India, there are several kinds of circular packs, some of which do look a little like ours, but experts believe that the Indians copied their cards from European ones, rather than the other way about.

All the cards we have described so far are the standard types which you can buy in the countries concerned. But in addition to these 'standard' packs, there are many hundreds of 'non-standard' packs. These are produced by various makers with all sorts of variations. Some have fanciful court cards, often very pretty, while others may be used to advertise products, with Kings and Queens holding beer mugs, or packets of some kind! Sometimes all the cards in the pack will have some kind of picture on them, apart from the usual suit-signs. Occasionally, the pack may be humorous, or some times used for propaganda, even to publicise some political theme. The most recent one in Britain was issued to commemorate the anniversary of the makers, Thomas de la Rue & Sons.

Opposite page: top row; from a fancifully-designed French pack, a pack from Germany with large numbers which can be used as a calendar, a new design from a pack issued by a German airline, and a Spanish pack in which the courts show Indians and the arts of North America. The four Queens in the centre row are: from a pack advertising a British tailors, a Russian card from a Jubilee pack, a German humorous pack, and an Ethiopian pack. The bottom row of Jacks are from: a Japanese humorous 'Western' pack, a Japanese local-design pack, a Belgian advertising pack for an aspirin firm, and a Japanese 'hunting and game' pack.
This page (from top to bottom): a Japanese pack with black courts and brightly-coloured figures, a modern design from France, an Arab-type Queen from a Russian pack, a humorous German design, and an East German pack, with courts based on an old design.

71

What do you think it would be like if there were no clocks or watches? You would not know what time to set out for school in the morning. You might arrive so early that there would be no one else there, or you might arrive so late that lessons would be half finished. You would have no idea when to go for a train or a bus, for you would not know what time they were running.

In the old days, before there were clocks, people invented all kinds of ways of telling the time. They were not usually very accurate, but they were better than nothing.

The top picture on the left shows a "scratch dial," which was used in Medieval times. It was like a sundial, drawn on a stone wall. It was divided into twelve, for the twelve hours of the day and anyone wanting to know the time pushed a piece of stick into the hole in the middle. The place where the stick's shadow fell showed the time of day.

The preacher in the next picture has a different kind of clock to tell him how long to preach. This is a sand clock. Sand was put into a glass with a narrow neck and allowed to run through into another glass at the bottom. This clock could be used a second time by turning the glass upside down and letting the sand run back again, but it was only useful for measuring small amounts of time such as five, ten or fifteen minutes. The largest convenient size for a sand clock was one which measured sixty minutes and was called an hour-glass. We still use a small version of the sand clock for timing boiled eggs.

It was possible to tell the time at night just by looking at the light. Look at the candle in the lantern and you can see that it is divided

The "scratch dial" used in Medieval times, seen top left, was a sundial scratched on a stone wall. To know the time you put a stick in the hole in the centre and watched where the shadow fell. For timing short periods an hour-glass was used (centre-left).

Candles and oil lamps had the hours marked on them. As they burnt away, you could tell the time.

upon a time...

into rings. There were twelve or twenty-four rings and as the candle burnt down you could tell the hour by counting the number of rings still left. Oil lamps, too, had the hours marked on the side. As the lamp burned, the level of the oil showed the time. Candles and oil lamps were not very accurate, because some candles were thicker than others and oil lamps did not always burn steadily.

A sundial was more accurate, for as the sun moved across the sky, the shadow of the metal hand moved around the sundial, showing the exact time of day. In Tudor times, people had a special little sundial which they could carry around in their pockets, as well as the ones in their gardens. However, sundials were no use at night, or when the weather was bad and there was no sun.

Nobody knows who invented clocks with weights, like the big Victorian grandfather clock in the picture, but they may have reached England hundreds of years ago in the time of the Crusaders. However, it was only when clocks and watches could be made quickly and cheaply by machines, that everyone could afford to buy them.

Sundials were very useful for telling the time in fine weather, but they were useless at night, or when there was no sun. The first clocks were big ones, probably brought to England six or seven hundred years ago. It was not until Tudor times that small clocks and watches, which could be carried in the pocket, were invented. Even in Victorian times, most families still had tall grandfather clocks like the one shown.

SIGNS OF

Most of Nevada, the seventh largest of America's union of States, is desert. With so much sand about and with its neighbours, like California and the big farm country of Idaho, attracting so much attention, Nevada has to be different.

And indeed, nothing could be quite so different as Nevada and particularly its largest, wildest town, Las Vegas.

The tourists who come in their hundreds of thousands every year do not come to see ancient buildings or old masters in picture galleries. They come to gamble – and Las Vegas caters for them in the grand manner.

In 1931 the State of Nevada legalised gambling and for Las Vegas, then a desert outpost of a few thousand people, the new law was the signal for an amazing expansion.

Down its wide main street, called 'the Strip', developers erected lines of luxurious casinos and hotels, some of which, like The Dunes, and The Sands, have become famous all the world over.

To these hotels, all equipped with large theatres, come the

"Come and have fun" plead the gay sig

LAS VEGAS

greatest entertainers in America – singers, comedians, film and variety stars. They play to capacity houses of tourists eating their dinner – which provides a relaxed break from the serious business of gambling.

Gambling is a non-stop, 24-hour pursuit in Las Vegas. The hotels on the Strip are equipped with hundreds of 'fruit machines', or 'one-armed bandits'. There is never any shortage of players despite the vast array of machines, sometimes as far as the eye can see. The steady drumming sound of levers being pulled is punctuated occasionally only by the metallic avalanche of coins which announces the arrival of a ten-dollar jackpot – the ultimate reward for all the forearm energy.

Tiring, perhaps, the lone gambler can leave his fruit machine to join a card table, a bingo session, or a roulette group. Nothing has been omitted.

No visitor can fail to be surprised on coming for the first time to Las Vegas, a town built for mass gambling in the middle of a parched and searing desert.

bait for those with money to burn

It's fun, fun, fun

all the way in gay

Las Vegas, if your

pockets are bulging

with dollar bills,

you have a fortune

at the bank and a

kind friend to lend

you the fare home

when you have lost

your last penny in

the glittering

casinos of this

gambling capital

of the U.S.A.

The first sound heard in the town's airport is that of one-armed bandits. The machines, in serried rows, reach right up to the passengers' arrival doors. It is easy to understand why Nevada's largest single source of State revenue, after sales tax, comes from gambling.

When the eyes have become accustomed to the glare — summertime temperatures touch 120 degrees Fahrenheit, though all the gamblers operate in air-conditioned comfort — the first impression of the Strip is a bewildering collection of brightly coloured signs vying for the visitors' attention, and his dollars.

The signs announce hotel comforts, easy money to be made by gambling, what's for breakfast, and the current visiting star attraction.

Occasionally they announce a wedding place for, unique among American States, Nevada has no residential qualification for prospective married couples. You can arrive in Las Vegas, walk right in to a chapel and get married, all within the space of a few minutes.

After only six weeks of residence in the State you can get a divorce, a short waiting period which has been capitalised on by Reno, another town which lies in the north of the State, across the arid desert which can be seen through the gaps in the signs as you walk down the Strip. The dictum 'married in Vegas, divorced in Reno' is frequently practised in the United States.

Today 70,000 people live in this desert valley town isolated by mountains. Most of them work in the hotels and casinos, where life never stops, not even during the normal hours of sleep. In Las Vegas man has built a unique monument to twentieth century leisure.

Behind the signs is a battle for business. Each tries to out-glitter its rivals in attracting customers to the gambling casinos and hotels of this town built on a desert in the American West. Customers are enticed from the outdoors heat by the promise of air conditioned interiors, free photographs and cheap food. But once inside, they get hooked on things like progressive jackpots that empty their pockets quicker than it takes a sign to flash on and off.

THE STORY OF THE
Red Indian

"If I were an Indian," wrote the glory-hunting general, "I think that I would greatly prefer to cast my lot among those of my people who adhered to the free open plains, rather than submit to the quiet, unexciting, uneventful life of a reservation."

General George A. Custer wrote those words not long before he lost his life, along with the rest of his command, at the Battle of the Little Big Horn in Montana one blazing day in June 1876. Nearly a century has gone by since that ferocious, hour-long fight, and over 80 years since the last of the Indian wars ended in a massacre of Sioux men, women and children at Wounded Knee by men of Custer's old regiment, the Seventh Cavalry. But still the imagination of the world is held by the story of how the Indians fought for so long against impossible odds.

Not that an Indian's life was all fighting, though most tribes were warrior societies. Strangely, when we think of an Indian, the first picture that comes to mind is a warrior on a horse somewhere on the Great Plains of the United States; yet there were no horses in America when the first Indians crossed the Bering Strait between Asia and Alaska, which was then a land bridge, more than 30,000 years ago. They were later named wrongly by Columbus who thought he had reached the East Indies on his great voyage of 1492. As for "Redskins", the first Indians the whites saw in the East had lightish skins which, when tanned by the sun, became copper-coloured. Hence the name!

More and more tribes crossed into America down the centuries, some reaching the tip of South America. Others were the ancestors of those two greatest of Indian civilisations, the Incas of Peru

An Algonquin Medicine Man

On the warpath!

An Arapaho ritual dance

victims to gain their strength.

Farming was widely practised in the East, the women doing the work raising corn, potatoes, tobacco etc., when the men went hunting. Much of America was covered with countless millions of buffalo, which gave the Indians food, shelter and clothing.

When the first settlers from England arrived in the early 16th century the Spaniards had already explored some of the southwest searching vainly for gold. They left horses behind whose descendants were the wild horses of the Plains. There must have been a wonderful moment when the first Indian rode and tamed one of them.

The Indians rapidly became some of the finest light cavalry in the world and their lives were transformed. The buffalo hunt was now fast, thrilling and efficient and war was more exciting than ever. It was typical of the Plains Indians that they counted it a greater honour to move in close, touch an enemy and retreat than to kill him.

Meanwhile, back East, the whites were busy driving the Indians westwards, except for a few left on reservations, or those dead from white diseases or bullets. The worst removals occurred in the 1820s and 30s when the Five Civilised Tribes,

and the Aztecs of Mexico, both conquered by the Spaniards in the 16th century.

We are only concerned here with the Indians of what became the U.S.A., Stone Age men when the whites arrived, hunting on foot, with dogs dragging their belongings. There were perhaps a million of them when Columbus reached the New World.

Some tribes, like the Iroquois, who lived in what is now New York State, and held the balance between France and England in the 18th century, were very advanced, with a fine democratic system of government; others, like the Diggers of California, grubbing for roots, were as backward as could be. But they shared certain things in common: they worshipped the Sun and also the Earth, which they never pretended to own. How could one own one's mother? They loved public speaking; they were kindly parents who adored their children; they were influenced by omens – good and bad "medicine" – and most of the men adored fighting.

Indians were cruel in war and they often tortured prisoners, just like many Europeans of those days. But Indians often admired those they tortured, honouring them if they sang defiantly at their captors. Some Indians ate the hearts of brave

Chief Cochise of the Apaches

Cherokees, Choctaws, Chickasaws, Creeks and Seminoles, were forced west to Indian Territory, now Oklahoma. They got their name because they had advanced so fast, outstripping many whites. A Cherokee named Sequoyah had actually invented an alphabet which made his entire people able to read and write. The envious whites forced them out, only a few surviving in the swamps of Florida and the hills of North Carolina.

Now it was the turn of the Plains Indians, romantic figures until the whites wanted their land when they became "painted savages". They watched settlers, gold-seekers, railroad builders and soldiers come and they fought when treaties were broken, even though the wisest of them saw that the whites were numberless. And the whites had better weapons, one use for their rifles being almost to exterminate the buffalo, which was the Indians' staff of life.

The Indians made a series of last stands. It was during this period that many of the great chiefs appeared: Red Cloud of the Sioux, Quanah Parker of the Comanches, the noble Joseph of the Nez Perces, who almost succeeded in leading his tribe to Canada and safety after an epic fighting retreat in 1877.

Custer's Last Stand was a victory right enough for the Sioux, Cheyennes and Arapahoes under

A Sioux warrior

A Pawnee Medicine Man

Crazy Horse, Gall and Sitting Bull, but it was the beginning of the end. Soon the victors were being rounded up on to reservations, usually land the whites did not want. A few smaller tribes like the Shoshonis, Pawnees and the Crows, who fought with the Americans against their Indian enemies, got slightly better reservations, but there was no more real freedom.

The fiercest wars of all were in the Southwest, where the fierce Apaches did not finally give up until 1886, after fighting under brilliant leaders like Cochise, Mangas Coloradas, Victorio and Geronimo. They could live in the desert like lizards, run 40 miles a day, and ride twice as much, and only by using Apache scouts did the U.S. Army find them, let alone fight them.

Today, some Indians make good, like those Apaches who are cowboys and the Mohawks who build skyscrapers, having no fear of heights. Individuals do brilliantly, but many, trying to lead a communal life on their often pitiful reservations, lead sad lives. Many who go to the cities lack the education to succeed, though in Oklahoma the Indians are very much part of the life of the state. But there is a new pride in today's Indians to match that of their ancestors. Things are looking brighter for these ever fascinating first Americans.

The last of the
SAILING SHIPS

Air billowed the sails of the three-masted sailing ship. Deck hands could hear the canvas flapping angrily as the wind whistled through the rigging, and the masts creaking protestingly as they strained against the deck.

In his cabin, the skipper looked up from his charts, and turned to the First Mate who was beside him.

"If we don't play out the shore lines, we'll rip away the bollards," the skipper said. "Are we ready to sail?"

The mate nodded. "Cargo's all stowed. The wind and tide are favourable. What do you reckon of the other clippers, sir?"

"They're fine vessels," mused the skipper. "But we'll show 'em a clean pair of heels, all the way to England."

Opening the door of his cabin, the skipper stepped on to the deck to look at his competitors. There were four other sailing ships, either tied up at the jetty or anchored amidstream in China's Foochow harbour. All were waiting for the right moment to set sail for England, and each wanted to get there first.

These were tea clippers, fine vessels of the mid-nineteenth century with sleek lines for fast speeds. If their freight space was small, this did not matter for the cargo they carried was worth a good deal in London. But it had to be got there quickly to fetch the best price and to keep its quality. A premium of a £1 a ton was paid to the owner of the ship arriving with the first of the season's tea. Consequently, there was always keen competition among the clipper captains to be the first arrival in London.

First Underway

As he watched, the skipper saw one of these ships, the *Taeping* cast off its shore lines and make ready for sailing. On the other ships, sailors were shinning up the masts to set the sails. Soon, they too would be heading out to sea.

Swiftly, the skipper gave orders to get his ship underway. Almost at once, the deck was bustling with activity as men pulled at tarred ropes to raise such yards as were not already in position. On the quayside, Chinese coolies released the ship's ropes from the bollards, and the beautiful ship began slipping out to sea. The race was on.

The date was 1866. The clipper was the *Ariel* and its skipper was determined to shoot ahead in the exciting dash over thousands of miles of ocean. Unless his skill, and the tides and the winds, were at fault, he knew he would succeed.

These clippers were the last of the fast sailing ships. Steam was coming to take their business away. But before that happened, the clippers were to go down in history as the fastest sailing ships of all times.

The most famous of them all was the *Cutty Sark*, now preserved at Greenwich, near London. This ship made many journeys from China in under a hundred days. Once, she sailed 350 miles a day for many days, a record which put the steamships of the time to shame.

It was an American who built the first clippers to carry mail from New York to Europe. Sailors refer to these early ships as semi-clippers, because they lacked the fine lines and underwater streamlining of the later models.

The first real clipper was the *Ann McKim* of Baltimore, which was built in 1832. Although this was a small ship which carried very little cargo, its high speed always assured it of plenty of freight.

In fact, it was this asset which made the clippers so successful. Businessmen who wanted to get their goods to their customers

The fo'c'sle, the crew's quarters, cramped, wet and shared with a winch!

The captain's cabin height of comfort on a square-rigger!

quickly, and were willing to pay for this service, found the clippers ideal.

Britain's clippers were first used to carry goods around the coasts. At this time, the monopoly of trading with China was held by the East India Company, and remained with them until 1832. After this date, the trade was open to all comers, and the ships that could guarantee to bring their cargo home at the fastest speed were the ones that got the business.

More and more people were drinking tea in Britain, and, apparently, they were wealthy enough to pay the astonishingly high price demanded for it. It is no wonder that the clippers were concentrated on the China tea run, which was so lucrative.

Faster Than Steam

With their slim hulls and enormous spreads of canvas of square yards and sails on all three or four masts, they whipped through the waves at 16 knots, outpacing the steamers which had first ventured on to the oceans in 1813. Even today, many cargo ships cannot equal this speed.

Another record is even more remarkable. This was achieved by a clipper called *Champion of the Seas* which averaged nineteen knots to cover 465 miles in a day.

But the clippers were at the mercy of the winds. They could be becalmed in still seas, while their skippers stalked furiously up and down the deck.

American Origin

The clipper was an American invention and, for a while, it was used to carry opium in Chinese waters. Then, the Navigation Acts, which had stopped American ships from bringing tea to Britain, were relaxed, and many fast passages resulted.

Bigger profits drew the Americans away from this to the passenger trade in America when, during the Californian gold rush, prospectors were willing to pay small fortunes to be taken speedily to the gold fields.

When this happened, Britain was left with the tea trade to itself, and did very well out of it. Later, the discovery of gold in New South Wales, Australia, brought fresh business for British clippers.

Wool then became an important Australian export. Be-

cause ships with bigger cargo holds were needed for this, the clippers were designed with fuller underwater bodies.

The opening of the Suez Canal in 1869, through which the clippers had to be towed, gave the steamers an advantage, because they would go through the canal under their own power.

If this robbed the clippers of the tea trade, they were still without competition in the carrying of Australian exports, where the lack of coaling stations kept out the steam ships.

Ariel and *Taeping* and their rivals in the passage from China to Britain were typical of the clippers of their day. Each was committed to a rival merchant in London, who wanted to get his tea on to the market ahead of his competitors. So the race between the vessels was real and in earnest.

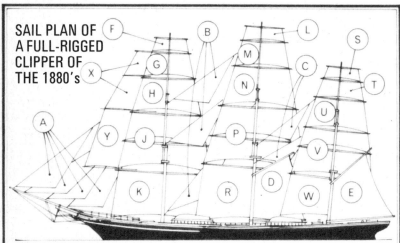

SAIL PLAN OF A FULL-RIGGED CLIPPER OF THE 1880's

Fore and aft sails: (A) (from bow) flying jib, outer jib, inner jib and fore topmast staysail; (B) (from top) main royal staysail, main topgallant staysail and main topmast staysail; (C) (from top) mizzen topgallant staysail and mizzen topmast staysail; (D) main spencer; (E) spanker.

Square sails: (F) fore skysail; (G) fore royal; (H) fore topgallant; (J) fore upper and lower topsails; (K) fore course; (L) main skysail; (M) main royal; (N) main topgallant; (P) main upper and lower top-

sails; (R) main course; (S) mizzen skysail; (T) mizzen royal; (U) mizzen topgallant; (V) mizzen upper and lower topsails; (W) crossjack.

Stunsails: (X) and (Y) show the position of three of the many stunsails which could be rigged on both the weather and lee sides of the ship. Each stunsail's position was indicated by prefixing it with "weather" or "lee" and adding the name of the sail, next to which it was rigged.

They had lost sight of each other after leaving Foochow, and it was not until they were in the English Channel that the crew of *Ariel* spotted the *Taeping* skimming along before a strong breeze.

At this, the competition became really keen. The rival skippers used all their skill in setting and resetting their yards and sails to get every ounce of speed out of the wind. And it was to tumultuous shouts of joy from the crew that *Ariel* sailed into her dock in London ten minutes ahead of the other clipper.

Ten minutes, after a journey of a hundred days or so over many thousands of miles, made it a tense and close victory. But it was one which enabled *Ariel's* merchants to grab the tea market's highest price and leave *Taeping's* dealers to scout around for any customers that remained.

In time, the glory of the days under canvas faded before the era of the smoky steamers, which were regular and reliable, but far less exciting successors to the sleek clippers and their billowing sails.

THE TYPEWRITER

The first really practical typewriter made its appearance a hundred years ago. But during the comparatively short period of time since then, it has completely revolutionised the clerical side of the world's business and has opened up worthwhile careers for millions of men, women and girls.

The first typewriter capable of practical work was the "typographer" which was patented by American inventor W. A. Burt of Detroit, in 1829. It was a cumbersome machine constructed mainly of wood, and ink had to be applied to an inking plate at frequent intervals. Although it could type capital and small letters, numerals and punctuation marks, it failed to reach the production stage.

A further advance came about in 1843, when Charles Thurber, of Worcester, Massachusetts, patented a machine having the first roller

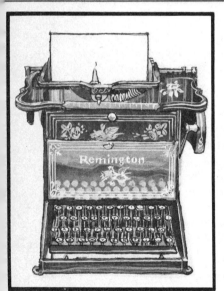

This is the machine that Sholes designed and Remington manufactured. Known as the Remington No. 1, it was lavishly decorated with mother-of-pearl inlay. Its keyboard characters were arranged for maximum convenience.

The Moya Model 1 (above) represents the very beginning of the present extensive typewriter industry in Leicester. It was invented in 1902 by Hidalgo Moya, a Spanish-American who had much experience of typewriter manufacture in the United States of America.

Sixty years ago, the Imperial Model A (above) was a leading machine. As was the case with the majority of early typewriters, the design of this machine made it difficult for the typist to have a clear view of the work being produced.

ts invention
evolutionised the
world of commerce

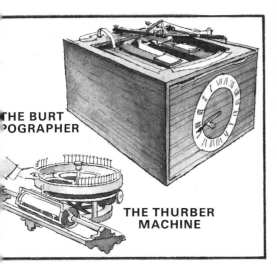

THE BURT TYPOGRAPHER

THE THURBER MACHINE

platen. The type characters were spaced out around the edge of a horizontal metal wheel, and each character was fixed to the lower end of a plunger.

To print a character on paper the wheel had to be rotated until the required character was in position and then the plunger had to be depressed.

The most important step in the development of typewriters was when Christopher Latham Sholes, a printer and inventor of Milwaukee, Wisconsin, began a series of experiments to produce a machine which would give trouble-free operation and high speed. He took out his first patent just one hundred years ago, in 1868. After further improvements, the well-known American sewing machine and small arms firm of Remington and Sons undertook production. The first commercial model appeared in 1873.

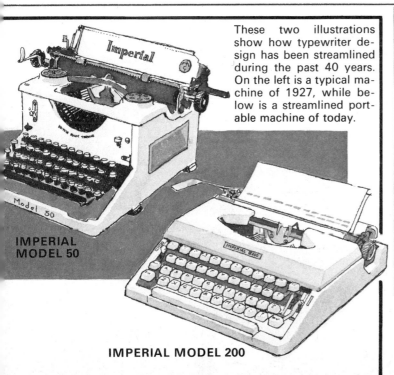

IMPERIAL MODEL 50

IMPERIAL MODEL 200

These two illustrations show how typewriter design has been streamlined during the past 40 years. On the left is a typical machine of 1927, while below is a streamlined portable machine of today.

Typewriters have been developed for use by handicapped persons.

This machine fitted with a specially designed keyboard, is being used by a spastic who is unable to use her hands fully.

PARACHUTES

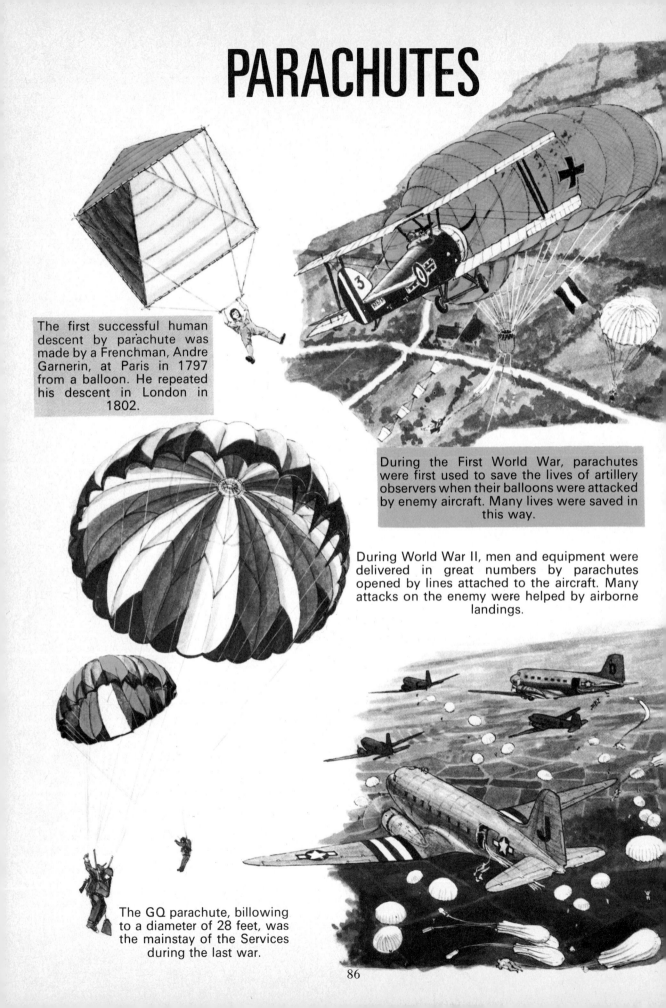

The first successful human descent by parachute was made by a Frenchman, Andre Garnerin, at Paris in 1797 from a balloon. He repeated his descent in London in 1802.

During the First World War, parachutes were first used to save the lives of artillery observers when their balloons were attacked by enemy aircraft. Many lives were saved in this way.

During World War II, men and equipment were delivered in great numbers by parachutes opened by lines attached to the aircraft. Many attacks on the enemy were helped by airborne landings.

The GQ parachute, billowing to a diameter of 28 feet, was the mainstay of the Services during the last war.

The Scorpion parachute (loft) is used in competitions and can be guided to land on a specially marked area on the ground.

Skydivers, like the one drawn above, fall freely before opening their parachute. Notice the clock and altimeter on his reserve parachute. The aerial antics of skydivers have thrilled thousands of people at air displays.

These three giant 83 feet in diameter red and white striped parachutes supported the Apollo Command Module when it splashed down after its half million mile journey to the Moon and back.

A precious boon to pilots of jet aircraft is the "ejector" seat, with parachute attached. When the pilot pulls a lever, an explosive charge is fired shooting the pilot and his seat and parachute away from the crashing aircraft.

High speed jet aircraft, when coming in to land, can be slowed down very quickly by means of a brake parachute.

BIRTH OF A MASTER BUILDER

For two, long, health-shattering years, work had slowly progressed on the building of the Thames Tunnel. The foul air under the river had stricken many of the engineers and miners with fever and blindness. And there was always the danger that water would break into the tunnel and claim even more victims.

The project was under the direction of a French engineer, Marc Brunel, and his English-born son, Isambard.

When work was begun on the tunnel, between Rotherhithe and Wapping, in 1825, Isambard laid the second brick, and the eighteen-year-old engineer was never far from the huge iron tunnelling shield which protected the miners during their excavations.

Isambard worked for up to thirty-six hours without sleep, and then would only take a brief nap behind the shield. One of his three assistants died of fever, and the other became partially blind.

Then, on the night of May 18th, 1827, Isambard heard a fearful shout from one of the miners working near the shield. A moment later, the shout was drowned by the thunder of water as the river suddenly came gushing in.

The miners threw down their tools and ran towards the foot of the shaft. Isambard, together with most of his men, managed to scramble safely up the shaft as the water roared past.

The young engineer was climbing to the surface when he heard a feeble cry for help coming from down below. It was an old man called Tillett, who tended the pumps at the shaft bottom. Without wasting a second, Isambard grasped hold of a rope and slid down an iron support to the trapped man.

He found Tillett up to his waist in the swirling water. Isambard quickly tied the rope around the man's waist. A few seconds later, Tillett and his rescuer were pulled to the surface.

After that, Brunel would have been entitled to take a long rest from tunnel-building, but the next day he was again at the bottom of the Thames, this time in a diving-bell, inspecting the damage. The bell was manoeuvred into the tunnel so that he could stand with one foot on the shield and the other on the newly-erected brickwork.

Adventurous Career

He seemed to be safely balanced, and one of his companions, a man called Pinkey, tried to follow his example. But as Pinkey straddled the shield and the brickwork, he lost his grip on the diving-bell and almost disappeared into the water-filled tunnel. Isambard immediately stretched out his leg so that Pinkey could seize hold of it. Then, making a superhuman effort, the engineer hauled the desperate man back into the diving-bell.

And then, as though that were not enough, Isambard had another near escape a few months afterwards when, in January, 1828, the tunnel collapsed again and drowned six miners.

Isambard Brunel was born in Portsmouth in 1806, but his family soon moved to London. Young Isambard wanted to be an engineer like his father. His ambition was to become Britain's "first all-round engineer and an example to future ones." To achieve this, he competed for the contract to build a bridge over the River Avon at Bristol. His design was accepted, and in June 1831, work began on the Clifton Suspension Bridge, which Brunel called "my first child."

In March, 1833, Brunel was appointed Engineer to what came to be called the Great Western Railway.

At a salary of £2,000-a-year, he overcame innumerable technical and engineering difficulties to forge the line between London and Bristol. The project cost £6½m. to complete; and the first train ran from Paddington to Bristol in June 1841.

With many feats behind him, he next turned his genius to the question of crossing the Atlantic by steamboat. He designed the famous *Great Western*, named after his beloved railway.

The steamboat first put to sea on March 28th, 1838, but on her maiden voyage, the underside of her deck caught fire while she was off Leigh-on-Sea, at the mouth of the Thames. For twelve hours Brunel helped to fight the fire.

Despite this inauspicious beginning, the *Great Western* steamed "magnificently" into New York harbour on April 22nd.

Brunel followed this triumph by designing an even larger steamboat, the *Great Eastern*, which at 700 feet long, and weighing 32,000 tons, was six times bigger than any other ship afloat. The *Great Eastern* was launched at Millwall on January 31st, 1858, and in September that year Brunel sailed with her on a trial voyage to Weymouth.

But years of unremitting work had taken their toll of the engineer. On September 5th, 1859, he had a stroke and collapsed on the *Great Eastern's* deck. He was left partially paralysed, and died ten days later.

Hell below zero

...all began at Stromness Bay in South ...eorgia, a dependency of the Falkland ...ands, and the last outpost of ...vilization before the eternal desolation ...the South Pole. The date was ...ecember 5th, 1914.

I cannot persuade you not to go, then, Mr Shackleton?

No! We have waited long enough!

Please take care. The whalers say that the weather is terrible in the Weddel Sea at this time of the year.

I know. But at least we all know what we are up against. Goodbye, Mr Sorlle.

So the ship called the 'Endurance' left Stromness Bay, carrying Ernest Shackleton's expedition of 28 men. Their objective was to undertake the first crossing of the Antarctic continent.

In the Weddel Sea, the weather was indeed terrible. Slowly, the ice began to close in around the 'Endurance.'

There is no point now in us staying with the ship. Everyone on land!

The ship drifted ever further south-wards for many months before it was finally abandoned on the 27th October, 1915.

Realising it was now impossible for them to reach the Pole, they began the long trek back to Stromness Bay.

They took with them the ship's bo
filled with stores, and these they
hauled on sledges. Eventually, the
reached Elephant Island, just as the
icefloes were beginning to break up
Quickly, they took to the boats.

As soon as he landed on the island, Shackleton realised they could never survive there for any length of time.

It's no good! Some of us must try and make it in one of the boats, while the others stay here.

There are ample supplies for all until a rescue party is brought back here.

But, Commander, the chances are a thousand to one!

I know that. But we have no other choice.

Later that day, Shackleton set off some of the others the launch named t 'Caird.'

Good luck, Captain!

Don't worry. I'll be back.

Their voyage was a terrible one, for at that time in the year, those seas were the roughest in the world.

They sailed 800 miles, braving monstrous waves and high winds.

And at last, on May 10th, 1916, they landed in South Georgia . . .

We must keep going at all costs.

Once we've reached the top of this, it's downhill all the way to Stromness Bay . . .

They were now climbing what seemed to be the last mountain.

The summ at last ! E we must scend bef the night comes. I we don't, the cold most certainly kill us !

They began their descent to the valley below.

But suddenly Shackleton realised something . . .

We're never going to reach the valley before nightfall.

That's a cheerful thought.

What do we do, then ?

I suppose all we can do is to just keep going.

That's not good enough ! We'll slide down !

You can't be serious ! We don't even know where we' end up !

True enough. But either we take the chance, or we die of the cold.

They prepared to face the unknown. First they made a kind of a seat out of the coil rope. Then they sat down or it, one behind the other.

Then they were on their way into the dark abyss below . . .

92

So far — so good!

Downwards, ever downwards they sped, gathering speed with every second.

One thought was in all their minds. Death could be lying in wait for them below. Perhaps even within the next few feet.

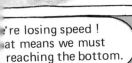

We're losing speed! That means we must be reaching the bottom.

They were now on a lower level, and a little more sheltered from the mortal cold. But they still could not stop. The journey continued in the moonlight.

They came to a sudden halt in a flurry of snow.

Is everyone all right?

Yes — it looks like we've made it, Commander!

I — I can go no further. Please — just ten minutes rest, Commander.

Very well. But you must stay awake. Otherwise you'll die where you're lying.

But despite Shackleton's warning, two of them fell asleep almost immediately.

The fools! They know that sleeping means freezing to death! But I suppose they're too tired to even care about that.

Wake up! Wake up, both of you!

the crossing of
South Georgia
in May 1916

South
Georgia

omness Bay ! Their incredible
ular journey was over at last !

Elephant Island
April 1916."

voyage of the
James Caird

Stromness
Bay, 15th
December,
1914 .

Palmer
Peninsula

route over the
pack-ice from
October 1915 –
April, 1916

pack ice broken
into icefloes

here the ice finally
stopped the Endurance
in October, 1915

sea frozen into
solid pack ice

voyage
of the
Endurance

N

S

Stromness Bay,
e workers were
king their way to
e factory as they
d every morning.

Look —
look over
there !

When . . .

Men — coming
from the direction
of the mountains !

We'd better get
over to them.
They look as
if they need
help.

Please —
please take
me to Mr.
Sorlle.

They were indeed
all in sore
need of help.

Of
course !

95

Excuse me, Mr. Sorlle. There is someone to see you.

What are you talking about man?

Sorlle's jaw dropped as he saw the figure who staggered into his room.

YES - IT'S ME - SHACKLETON...

After he had recovered fro[m] his ordeal, Shackleton led four relief expeditions befo[re] he finally managed to rescu[e] the rest of his expedition from Elephant Island.

Ernest Shackleton failed in his attempt to cross the Antarctic. But the epic trek he had made with his companions had added yet another page to the annals of human endurance.

EARLY BIRDS

One of the most charming groups in the animal world, birds have interested mankind from earliest times. Their song, plumage and flight have given pleasure and inspiration to people all over the world.

The Phoenix was a mythical bird. Egyptians believed that the bird buried its father in a shrine at Heliopolis and it was supposed to revisit Egypt every 500 years. Others claimed that it died in Arabia but that a young Phoenix immediately sprang up. Yet others say it burned itself and a new Phoenix rose from the ashes and began a new life.

The story of the Pelican feeding its young on its own blood is said to have originated in Egypt. Many heraldic pictures show this bird pecking its breast to draw blood. This idea may have originated from the fact that Pelicans have red tips to their bills and often rest with them against their breasts.

Alexander the Great brought peacocks from India in 324 B.C. and they were kept at Samos as sacred to the goddess Hera. Each new moon, or Hera's day, the public were allowed to see them for a fee and could buy their eggs when in season. The Romans brought peacocks from Greece to Italy in the first century B.C. Nobles bred them for profit. Persian designers used peacock feathers as inspiration for the famous Peacock Throne which used to stand in the Imperial Palace at Delhi, India.

Philomela, daughter of Pandion, King of Athens, was turned into a Nightingale, and the bird appears in many Eastern legends. According to one, Solomon was told that the Nightingale kept other birds awake by his singing, but when the Nightingale told Solomon he sang for love of the Rose, Solomon forgave him and allowed him to continue singing.

As Christianity spread through Europe, many of the pagan religious beliefs about birds lingered on as superstition. For many centuries magpies were regarded as sacred in rural France, while in Britain the hoot of an owl was supposed to foretell evil. Sailors still dislike killing an albatross, believing that his death brings misfortune.

In many parts of Europe, particularly in Holland, people encourage Storks to breed by placing boxes on roof-tops for them. Good luck followed where the Storks nested and children were told that Storks carried new babies into homes. The return of the Storks was a sign of Spring, to be celebrated.

Fishermen in the Far East have for centuries made use of Cormorants. They train them to bring the fish they catch back to their masters. A ring round the Cormorant's neck prevents the bird from swallowing any fish.

Ravens have lived in the Tower of London since William the Conqueror's time. Tradition says the Crown will fall if they vanish, so replacements are constantly made. One wing is clipped to avoid escape. The six ravens in the Tower today are allowed a weekly meat ration and they prove a great attraction to visitors. They are friendly and seem to like meeting the public. Ravens were known to man in Biblical and even earlier times.

Today bird sanctuaries safeguard many species. Scientists ring birds to check their numbers and routes of migration, while aircraft designers have gained much help from the study of bird flight.

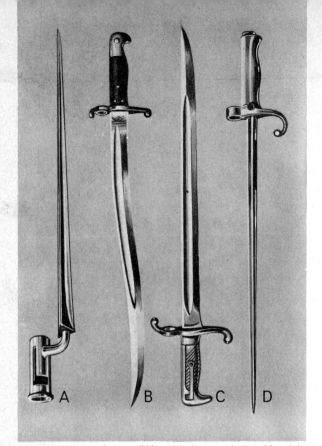

A A socket bayonet of about 1800, which slips over the barrel foresight and locks.

B A Yataghan bayonet used by many European armies in the middle of the 19th century.

C Mauser rifle brass hilted bayonet, about 1875.

D A French Lebel bayonet with a cross-section blade used in the First World War.

E Short Lee Enfield No. 1 Mk. III bayonet, standard equipment for British infantrymen at the beginning of the Second World War.

F Lee Enfield No. 4 Mk. I spike bayonet, introduced at the beginning of the Second World War, gradually replacing the No. 1 Mk. III.

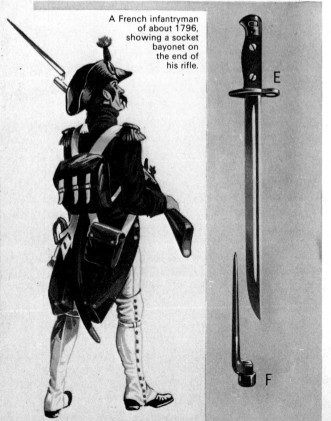

A French infantryman of about 1796, showing a socket bayonet on the end of his rifle.

BAYONNE

This French town gave its name to a deadly war weapon – the bayonet

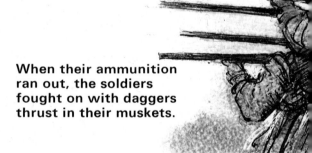

When their ammunition ran out, the soldiers fought on with daggers thrust in their muskets.

Bayonne, a French town four miles from the Bay of Biscay, was once famous for the elaborate scrolls and twirls wrought by its iron foundries. But since about 1650 its name has become known in every country where "bayonet" is part of the language.

A bayonet is a short stabbing weapon which is fixed to the muzzle of a rifle for hand-to-hand fighting. The earliest written record of their use is in the memoirs of a Bayonne-born commander named Puységur. He said that his troops, while fighting in 1647 at Ypres in Belgium, had thrust daggers, made at Bayonne, into the muzzles of their muskets after firing and, thus equipped with "bayonets," were able to fight on.

The first English bayonet was made in 1663 and consisted of a broad blade like a spear-head, with sword edges, so that it could be used for thrusting as well as cutting. Because its tapering wooden handle could fit into the end of the muzzle, this was called a plug bayonet.

a place with a point to it!

Early in the 18th century, guns were made with sockets so that the bayonet could be attached outside the barrel, enabling the musket to be fired with the bayonet fixed.

Throughout the 18th and 19th centuries, the bayonet was frequently altered to suit varying types of firearms, or to enable fresh ideas as to its use to be tried out.

Until the 20th century, some British rifle and light infantry regiments were equipped with bayonets which were actually short swords, capable of being fitted to rifles or wielded by hand.

Bayonets, it was thought, would become obsolete with the development of long-range, rapid-firing rifles. However, the hand-to-hand fighting in the trenches during the First World War proved their value.

Throughout that war, and during the early part of the Second World War, the standard British bayonet was a sword-edged weapon 17·2 in. long and weighing 1 lb. 2 oz.

The standard French bayonet was longer and more of a thrusting weapon. The typical Russian bayonet was triangular in shape and had no cutting edge because it was intended solely for thrusting.

In contrast, the Japanese used sword-bayonets on their light machine-guns.

A short 8·5 in. bayonet was adopted by the British army in 1942. This had no hilt, but a single ring fixture for attaching it to the rifle.

There were two types: the skewer and the fluted. Both were strictly thrusting weapons and, at close quarters, could be seized by an enemy. After the Second World War, the British army adopted a sword-edged, hilted bayonet 8·5 in. long.

Some early bayonets were so badly made that soldiers used them at their peril. In 1886, when British troops were trying to stop a revolt which had broken out among desert tribes in the Sudan, in Africa, many bayonets were bent and twisted in charges. After this, they were carefully tested before being issued to soldiers.

The Burlington Zephyr

America's first main line express diesel

In May, 1934, Chicago was thronged with people. Many of them, Americans and foreigners, were visiting the huge World Fair which was being held there. On the evening of 26th May, a big pageant was held and crowds flocked to watch it.

But, exciting as the pageant was, eyes kept turning to a temporary railway track which had been laid in the fairground.

Just as the pageant reached its climax, the sound of a diesel's horn was heard. Amid cheering and shouting, a three-coach diesel train entered the fairground.

The diesel had made a non-stop run from Denver to Chicago, a distance of over a thousand miles. The best steam trains took twenty-six hours to make this run. But the president of the railway company owning the diesel claimed that it would do the journey in half the time.

There was great excitement. Farmers lined the track to watch as the diesel train crossed the prairies, reaching a speed of 112 miles an hour. It did the journey in the time predicted – just over thirteen hours.

Its success meant that the age of steam was to pass. For forty years, the steam engine fought for survival. But the outcome was inevitable. Gradually diesel trains began to replace them.

Even so, in 1934 the diesel engine was not a new invention. It was named after the German engineer who invented it, Rudolph Diesel, who was born in 1858.

Diesel realised that in steam engines, only a small part of the heat which could be produced from the fuel was actually used. So he began to experiment, trying to make engines work more efficiently.

What is the difference between a diesel and an ordinary petrol engine?

A petrol engine has a mixture of air and petrol sucked into the cylinder, and this is ignited by a sparking plug.

A diesel engine sucks air into the cylinder, and the up-stroke of the cylinder compresses the air to 500 to 600 pounds a square inch. This creates a high temperature in the cylinder head.

Diesel fuel is then injected at a pressure of about 1,000 pounds a square inch (sometimes more) and is ignited as a result of the high temperature of the compressed air. There is no spark in a diesel engine.

The first engines they devised were extremely heavy and suitable only as industrial stationary engines used in factories. Others with increased power, although still heavy, were suitable for use in ships.

Eventually, as stronger metals became available, it was possible to make engines light enough to be used in railway locomotives, heavy lorries, buses and even cars.

When the diesel train made its record breaking run in 1934, a depression had hit the railways as more people took to travelling by car. But the diesels gave the railways new life. Diesels cost more to build than steam engines, but they are cheaper to run, faster, give a smoother ride and do not need servicing so often. As a result, they have helped the railways to reduce their costs.

Although some publicity is being given to turbo-jet driven locomotives today, they are only suitable for long distance, high-speed work, and we are likely to see conventional diesels in use on the railways for a very long time to come.

Other engineers, also aware of the shortcomings of the steam engine, had been experimenting with gas and heavy oil engines with limited success.

However, after several years' work, Diesel demonstrated an improved engine he had made, at Augsburg in Germany. But it exploded and nearly killed him.

Diesel started again, and this time he experimented with an engine using oil, instead of coal gas, which he had used before. This engine was a success and it was called a diesel engine, after its inventor.

Unfortunately, Diesel did not live to see his invention triumph as a form of transport. In 1913, he disappeared from a Harwich steamer during a journey across the English Channel. Others, however, were ready to work on his engine and find ways of improving it.

A sailor aboard the Trinity House supply boat signalling to the keepers of the present-day Eddystone lighthouse.

THE LIGHTHOUSE THAT VANISHED

Henry Winstanley was very proud of his lighthouse. But even his masterpiece could not withstand a raging tornado.

Henry Winstanley was an unusual man. He was an artist and designed playing cards. He lived far from the sea, but he became famous for building the first Eddystone lighthouse.

Eddystone Rock juts from the waters of the English Channel right in the path of ships making for Plymouth. Its jagged edges can be seen above the water on a clear, calm day, but on a stormy night they are often covered by waves, and many times a sea captain's first hint of the rock was when it ripped the bottom of his boat.

During the reign of King William III it was decided to build a lighthouse on the rock. Henry Winstanley decided to take on the difficult task with the help of Admiralty boats and men.

It took all of one summer to make twelve holes in the rock into which iron bars were fixed. In the next two years a wooden lighthouse was built around the iron rods and huge tallow candles were set burning in the main gallery.

Henry Winstanley was very proud of his lighthouse, especially when it withstood the storms of its first winter without damage. At times the sea had lashed higher than its weather vane. During the next summer he improved and enlarged the building to 120 feet.

It was Winstanley's wish to be inside the lighthouse during the strongest storm known, just to see how well it would stand up to the battering.

On the night of Friday 26th November 1703, he was granted this wish . . .

For some three weeks there had been storms and constant bad weather. Then a day of calm before the weather broke up again. Sensing a fierce storm; Winstanley took a boat on the Friday afternoon and went out to his lighthouse.

That night there was a storm. Not just an ordinary storm, or even a very bad one. This was the night of the Great Storm, a night when the wind roared with such violence that it sounded like continual thunder. It was the night when church steeples crashed to the ground, windmills were stripped of their sails and toppled over like skittles. Oak trees and fruit trees alike were snapped and uprooted by tens of thousands. Chimney stacks crashed down through roofs, houses collapsed, some were even lifted up and blown away. Men and women were blown out of bed and buried in falling rubble. Thousands of sheep and cattle were drowned in river floods. Ships were battered and heaped one upon the other in rivers and harbours. Seamen, townsmen and countrymen perished in the terrifying disaster.

People hid in cellars praying, for they thought the world was at an end. It was pitch black. There was no moon, not even lightning. There was noise, the thundering wind, the crashing of broken trees and the deadly rattle of roof tiles skimming through the air to hit other buildings with the force of explosives.

For the first and only time a tornado, such as cause terrible havoc in parts of America, escaped across the Atlantic, gathered strength on the way and passed across Southern England and parts of Europe.

Those trembling people who crawled from their ruined homes on Saturday morning and looked towards the Eddystone lighthouse saw the rock and a few twisted fingers of iron sticking up.

The lighthouse, its creator and all those in it had vanished without trace – for not even Henry Winstanley had foreseen the fury of the Great Storm.

A huge rocket, as big as a skyscraper, stands on its launching pad at Cape Kennedy, U.S.A. High in its nose, in their space capsule, sits a team of three astronauts, braced for take-off.

On their headphones, they can hear the curt commands of the mission controller, as he supervises the various checking procedures which must be gone through before the mighty rocket soars into the air on its tail of fire.

In a dull monotone, he begins the count-down.

"Ten . . . nine . . . eight . . ."

An intense silence descends upon the mission control headquarters. The scientists sit, with taut nerves, at their dials and display panels, watching flickering needles and dancing bleeps on cathode ray tubes.

All over the world, people are glued to their television sets, watching the space monster with its sharp nose silhouetted against the sky.

A strange expectancy fills the air, for this is no ordinary mission. It is the first mission to that mysterious red planet far out in the universe . . . Mars.

The countdown is nearly over.

"Three . . . two . . . one. Ignition. We have lift off."

With a roar as loud as that of a hundred jet planes, the amazing rocket thunders off on its historic journey to the planet on which man has never set foot.

What will they find there? Will they encounter strange forms of Martian life

The planet Mars as it appears through a telescope situated on the earth. This picture was taken at Catinia Observatory in Sicily.

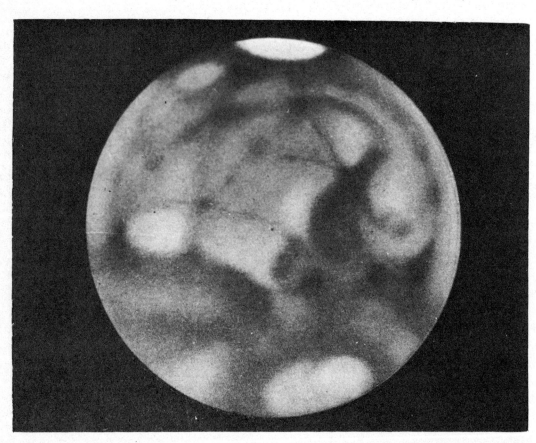

NEXT STOP MARS

When Man steps on to the Martian surface for the first time, perhaps in the 1980s, he may find himself lumbering over rocky land rather like the Moon's. Or he may make discoveries which will be so startling that they astound the world.

which have developed in the planet's peculiar atmosphere?

We may not know the answers to these, and many other questions which fill our minds about Mars, until America sends astronauts to this planet in the 1980s.

But before this can happen, the plan is to make a thorough exploration of the planet with orbiting space craft which will be unmanned. While they are encircling Mars, these craft will launch smaller craft, covered with a protective shell to protect the landing craft inside from heat built up by the descent in the thin Martian atmosphere of carbon dioxide.

When they get within the pull of Mars' gravity, the shells will open and release the landing craft with its parachute, retro-rockets and landing legs.

From Earth, scientists will control the descent of the landing craft, opening the parachutes and firing the retro-rockets when necessary to ensure that the vehicle makes a soft landing.

Once it is on the Martian surface, which is expected to be like that of the Moon, metal prongs will scoop up samples of soil and draw them into the craft, where automatic devices will start analysing them.

Their findings will be radioed back to Earth together with television pictures of the rugged terrain. If these indicate that man could safely set foot on the planet, the first manned trip could take place in 1981.

For this, two atomic spaceships would be assembled in earth-orbit, each with a crew of six. Rocket stages would start the vehicle on its journey around the sun to meet Mars in its orbit. When they get near to Mars, the space ships will separate and fire their nuclear engines to go into an orbit around Mars for ninety days. From each vehicle, three men would go down to Mars in their landing craft to explore the surface for thirty days.

It will take about nine months to get to Mars in actual flight time. But the journey must be backed by years of planning and research. And if it fails, Man will not get another chance to go there until 1986, when Mars will be in a suitable position again.

Mars, with its polar caps of carbon-dioxide snow, no liquid water and no canals, such as for long were believed to exist, may be as barren and desolate as the Moon. But, on the other hand, it may possess secrets that can startle the world.

A close-up of Mars. One of the thousands of photographs of the surface of Mars taken by Marina 9 and radioed back to earth. It shows a valley 250 miles long and three or four miles wide.

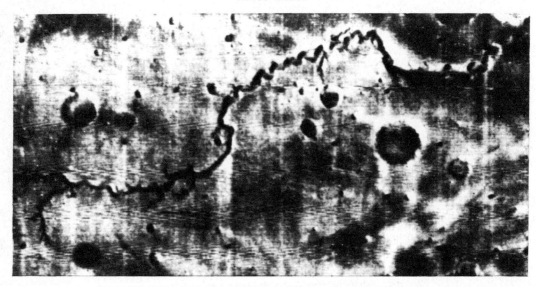

THE 'ROYAL' STAR GAZER

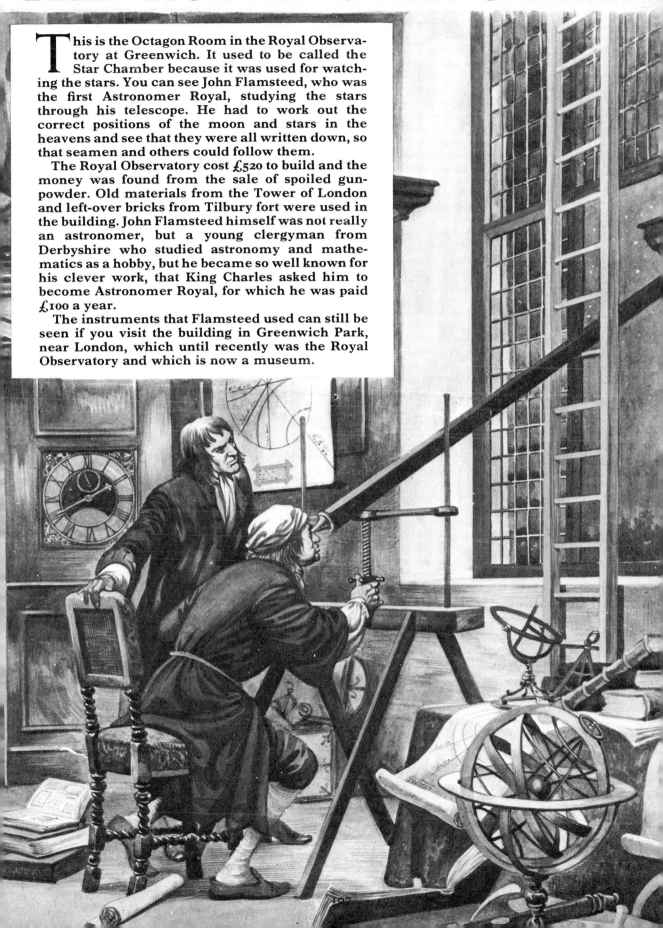

This is the Octagon Room in the Royal Observatory at Greenwich. It used to be called the Star Chamber because it was used for watching the stars. You can see John Flamsteed, who was the first Astronomer Royal, studying the stars through his telescope. He had to work out the correct positions of the moon and stars in the heavens and see that they were all written down, so that seamen and others could follow them.

The Royal Observatory cost £520 to build and the money was found from the sale of spoiled gunpowder. Old materials from the Tower of London and left-over bricks from Tilbury fort were used in the building. John Flamsteed himself was not really an astronomer, but a young clergyman from Derbyshire who studied astronomy and mathematics as a hobby, but he became so well known for his clever work, that King Charles asked him to become Astronomer Royal, for which he was paid £100 a year.

The instruments that Flamsteed used can still be seen if you visit the building in Greenwich Park, near London, which until recently was the Royal Observatory and which is now a museum.

THE DEATH OF AN

AIRSHIP

Inside the control car of the airship *Hindenburg*

In these modern days of jumbo-jets we think of airships as the prehistoric monsters of the air.

They were huge, bigger than even the biggest jumbo-jets, slow and, like the huge and slow prehistoric monsters, they are all dead and gone.

Only Germany had any real success with airships. This was thanks to two men. One was the nobleman Count von Zeppelin, who spent a lot of money building early airships. The other was the clever engineer and airship captain Hugo Eckener. Forty-one years ago Hugo Eckener flew an airship with a full load of passengers right around the world. Starting from New York he stopped only at Germany, Japan and on the Pacific coast of America.

In those days it was more than any aeroplane could do.

Afterwards this airship *Graf Zeppelin* and a sister ship *Hindenburg* made regular flights across the Atlantic Ocean, direct from Germany to South America and then to Lakehurst, New Jersey, a landing field not many miles from New York.

Travelling by airship was smooth and comfortable, and although airships built or owned by Britain and America had crashed and ended up in terrible disasters, these two great German ships flew many thousands of miles in perfect safety, until one Thursday evening in May, 1937.

The *Hindenburg* was ending a passenger flight from Germany by way of South America dead on time over Lakehurst. It was a stormy evening. There had been some thunder, but the storm clouds were moving away.

The great airship was moving slowly towards the tall iron tower to which its nose would be moored. Long ropes had already been lowered to the ground for teams of men to haul upon and steady the airship against the wind.

Then on top, near the upright fin at the back was seen a flame. It was not a very big flame at first, seen as it danced against the dark clouds. Then suddenly there was a mighty explosion as almost all the rear half of the airship caught fire at once. The silk fabric quivered and vanished in the heat. The metal girders within melted and bent. Flames rushed along the inside of the dying ship and flared from its nose. A terrible sight, the blazing airship broke almost in half and sank slowly to the ground.

It lay there burning until nothing remained but its twisted metal framework.

Thirty-five people had died within seconds. With them died the age of the airship for travellers were too frightened to fly in such dangerous things again.

Why did it happen? The cause remains a mystery. Some people thought an electrical spark or a flash of lightning caused the fire. Others say a time-bomb caused the disaster.

The airship was filled with a gas called hydrogen which burns very easily. This gas, which is lighter than air, was used to make the airship float above the ground.

There is another gas that is almost as light as hydrogen. It is called helium, and it cannot catch fire but the Germans did not have any safe helium so they used explosive hydrogen.

If helium had been used neither lightning nor a time-bomb could have caused the dreadful fire and the age of the smooth and almost silent airships may have lasted many more years – perhaps even to this very day.

BEAU BRUMMEL

It was, men declared unanimously, the finest cravat that had ever been tied. There had never been such a perfect knot; so elegant, so completely sophisticated. Admirers fell back in wonderment before the wearer of the cravat; hands went to mouths to hide astonished gasps and monocles dropped abruptly from raised eyes.

The cravat became the talk of London society. How had it happened, they asked each other breathlessly in the fashionable clubs? The war with France was forgotten as the cravat was discussed, dissected and deliberated upon.

Of one thing all were certain. George Bryan Brummell, the best dressed man in London, had perfected a cravat that put his title beyond the reach of mortal men.

Although the clubroom gossips did not know it, "Beau" Brummell as he was thereafter to be reverently called, had worked alone for days and nights to produce this latest piece of perfection in dress.

Age of Frippery

He had had scores of muslin cravats specially starched for his experiments. He had spent hours before his dressing room mirror contorting his chin and the muscles of his face to achieve the exact lie of the cravat, to form each perfect crease precisely. And if at any stage during the operation he had made an error, he had discarded the ruined muslin and begun all over again.

Beau Brummell positively slaved for his title as the number one dandy in London. And it wasn't a title anyone was going to be allowed to challenge.

Each morning Brummell took two hours to wash and shave and two hours to dress. Part of the shaving ritual was to pluck out with tweezers all those hairs that his razor had missed. He changed his shirt, he said, three times a day, and used the froth of champagne to shine his boots, which were polished by his valet on the soles and heels as well as the uppers.

While all this was going on, Brummell used a silver dish to spit in, for,

He had spent hours before his dressing room mirror, contorting his chin to achieve the exact lie of the cravat, to form each crease precisely.

he said, no gentleman could possibly spit in clay.

Brummell scorned travelling in a carriage because the smell of the horses offended his nose and because when the carriage stopped he might have to step down into mud. Instead he used an old-fashioned sedan chair, carried at each end by two flunkies, which took him right up to the door of his destination.

Although his dress was perfect – so perfect that Beau Brummell has earned a unique place in history simply for the way in which he turned himself out for the admiring London scene – there was much more that went to make the name of Brummell famous besides his magnificent cravat, his suit, his linen, boots and coat.

To begin with, Brummell actually washed. If that sounds an extraordinary statement, that is what it was in the Regency period.

The French Revolution, that greatest ever social upset in Europe, had exported some of its bad habits to England, not the least of which was the new French idea that only the unwashed lower classes were the salt of the earth. To wash in post-revolutionary France was to identify oneself with the old aristocratic regime; therefore not to wash was patriotic. And there were many in the circles of power in England who adopted this as a fashionable idea.

Besides washing, Brummell insisted that all his linen was spotless.

He made trousers a new mode of dress and introduced styles in boots that hundreds rushed to copy. He saw that his "props", like his silver snuff box, taken from his impressive collection of snuff boxes, were of the finest make, and even practised the perfect way to hold the box while delicately positioning the fingers to remove the snuff.

Besides all this well-practised polish, Brummell had the height, the handsome face, the fine figure and the elegance to carry off his dandy image. And he was a man born at the right time for frippery – at the time when the thin upper crust of Georgian England, living in their town clubs, madly gambling and furiously gossiping, had little better to do than admire the turn of a man's suit and the lie of his cravat.

It was an age when wit and repartee were worshipped, and Brummell shone at both. It was as an Eton schoolboy on holiday that he first came to the notice of the Prince of Wales, later Prince Regent and later still King George the Fourth. The Prince liked and encouraged witty young men for his idle courts at Brighton and London, and he promised to advance the cause of young George Brummell.

Brummell went to Oxford and then, with a considerable fortune left to him by his father, set out to ingratiate himself with the mindless Prince. His wit, elegance and sophistication made him the darling of

the Court and soon no ball or party, no society drawing room or aristocratic gathering, was complete without Beau Brummell, who consented to favour the occasion with his presence only if the guest list exactly suited him.

The whole of Brummell's life, and the lives of his peers in society, were centred around the arts of dressing perfectly, gossiping smartly and gambling foolishly. They did no work.

Decline of a Dandy

Even the dandy poet Lord Byron was impressed with this elegant age of English society. "There are but three great men in the nineteenth century," he said, "Brummell, Napoleon and myself. I would rather be Brummell than Napoleon."

The frolics centred around the Prince of Wales who, as the madness of his father King George the Third was confirmed, was appointed Prince Regent. The Prince soon took up with Mrs. Fitzherbert, whose common manners were not the kind which Brummell expected at Court.

When he made the fact too plain, the Prince's lady friend turned the Regent against the Court's favourite dandy. Society was agog when the Prince Regent deliberately "cut" Brummell at a party. Then the Beau took his revenge in a manner which rocked the gossips.

Passing down Bond Street, London, with a friend one day, Brummell met the portly, overweight Prince, who stopped to talk to Brummell's companion while studiously ignoring Brummell. When the conversation was terminated, Brummell was heard to remark in a loud voice to his companion: "Who is your fat friend?"

The remark was not surprisingly the final breach in Brummell's fading friendship with the Regent. "He is only fit to make the reputation of a tailor," hissed the Prince.

Without his Prince, Brummell was like a ship without a sail. No longer was he so welcome in the fashionable clubs; even less so when he began to borrow from the members sums of money, which he could not pay back, to cover his increasing gambling losses. In such a state a Georgian gentleman had only one recourse: to leave the country. In 1816, when he was 38 and crippled with debts, Brummell left England for France.

At Calais, where he lived, Brummell held his own "Court" for local French dignitaries and for society Englishmen passing through. They brought him the news of England and, because they were loyal to their class, they gave him gifts of money. In return, they enjoyed his wit, savoured his elegance and were permitted to watch the master of dan-

"Who is your fat friend?"

dyism at his two-hour washing and shaving ritual.

The price they paid for the sight of the sartorial master became an increasingly heavy one. Brummell continued to live as if money were water and expected everyone to support him. While the generosity of his friends seemed unbounded, his expenses continued to rocket. And when at last they demurred at the colossal expense of keeping the Beau, he treated them with cold disdain.

To one place-seeking creditor who asked diffidently if he could have the return of his £1,000 loan, Brummell snapped, "I have paid you already."

"When was that?" asked the creditor anxiously.

"When I leaned out of the window and said, 'Good morning, Jimmy,'" answered Brummell. The reply illustrates the mean, totally selfish attitude that characterised Brummell's life.

Brummell was saved temporarily from his rocketing debts by the death of King George the Fourth, who as Prince Regent had been his old mentor. Friends in London were at last able to find him a job, as British Consul in Caen. The salary was £400 a year, £320 of which Brummell was obliged before his departure to pledge annually to his Calais creditors.

With only £80 a year to live on, Brummell was doomed. Soon he owed money to everyone who mattered in Caen. Brummell wrote in despair to a government minister suggesting a transfer to a post with more work; whereupon the minister replied that no such post was vacant

and if there was insufficient work at Caen it would be better to dispense with the post. When Brummell was accordingly relieved of his job, his creditors closed in.

They were led by the bailiffs and within an hour Brummell found himself to his horror in the cell of a debtor's prison. Even there he managed to procure soap and a razor, and continued his ritualistic toilet before the astonished eyes of his fellow prisoners.

In London, the few aristocratic friends he had left rallied to Brummell yet again. Even the new King, William the Fourth, donated £100 to a fund to pay Brummell's creditors. And so, after 11 weeks in jail, he was released.

Brummell tried desperately to recapture his old life, but he was past it. Before his imprisonment he had suffered two minor strokes and prison life had left its mark on him. The friends who had paid his debts gave him a small income, but no income was sufficient for Brummell's tastes and way of life, and the shortage of funds made him a grey man. Now he could not even afford a clean shirt every day.

Gone was the dandy of yesteryear and in his place was an old, rough-bearded, feeble-minded man in tatters. In the streets people looked at him and nudged each other, whispering; the urchins laughed out loud. Slowly his mind became unhinged and sadly the last few months of a life that had been made famous by slavery to fashion were spent in a mental hospital.

TRAVELLING ABROAD

Journeying to distant places for holidays is quite a recent developme

Most of the people who travelled abroad in the Middle Ages were merchants, messengers, or pilgrims. Pilgrims journeyed to holy shrines and, like Chaucer's Canterbury pilgrims, they often rode in companies, singing and telling stories to pass the time.

Pilgrimages became less frequent after the Reformation, but 16th-century voyages were made by traders and adventurers like Hawkins, Drake and Raleigh. 17th-century religious differences caused whole communities to move. Long pleasure journeys were quite unknown.

The Grand Tour became an 18th-century fash After leaving school, rich young men would tra the Continent with tutors to complete their edu tion and broaden their outlook. They brought b works of art, and foreign ideas on architecture manners.

Literary men often travelled abroad to meet foreign writers. Milton visited Galileo in prison. Boswell called on Rousseau and Voltaire in Switzerland. Gibbon's visit to Rome is said to have inspired his great history "The Decline And Fall Of The Roman Empire".

During the French Revolution and Napoleonic wars, continental travel was not really practicable, but it began again soon afterwards. Until the coming of the railways, it was usual to take one's own stage coach abroad, for Continental coaches were not as good as the British.

In the mid-19th century, railways ma travel far easier. In 1839, Baedeker issu handbooks. In 1841, Thomas Cook ganised his first railway excursion in En land, which led to his first Continental t in 1855. Lower fares and better wa enabled more and more people to tra

Cook's tours first made travel possible for the middle classes. But the Victorians were critical of all things not English. They disliked foreign food. Even so, foreign travel began to extend its field as Polytechnic Tours and Lunn's Free Church Touring Guild made excursions cheaper.

As foreign travel became more possible for more people, the rich changed their holiday patterns. They bought their own Riviera villas and private yachts. Luxury cruises became fashionable. After the First World War passenger air services started and the more daring began to travel by air.

Since the Second World War, travel abroad become still more popular. Coach tours, ch flights, camping and touring by car have ope the world to everybody at reasonable prices. Common Market is making travel even easier w is a good thing in that it is making the British r cosmopolitan and tolerant.

Why it is called FOOLSCAP

FOOLSCAP PAPER is paper which usually measures 13½ inches by 17 inches, but often it is smaller. Nobody really knows how it got its name, although there are a number of theories.

Foolscap paper was in use in the mid-16th century and until the 17th century, foolscap paper made in Britain carried a watermark of a jester's head, with cap and bells. One story says that a German, Herr Spielmann, was the man responsible for introducing this watermark.

Spielmann settled in Britain, became a jeweller at Queen Elizabeth's court and changed his name to Sir John Spilman. He also opened the second paper mill in England and he wanted some kind of mark which would distinguish his paper from all the rest.

In German, *spielmann* means one who acts or plays, so Spielmann decided to put on his paper a head of a jester, a man who played the fool. Jesters were quite important people in the Middle Ages, being employed by nobles and royalty, so Spielmann used the jester's emblem, the cap and bells.

Another story attributes the jester's head watermark on foolscap to the conflict between King and Parliament in the 17th century. To raise money for his empty treasury, King Charles the First sold the monopoly to make various goods to the highest bidders. One of these goods was paper. The money from the sale of monopolies filled the royal treasury and so the king avoided calling Parliament.

At this time, paper bore the royal arms as a watermark, but when King Charles was defeated by the Roundhead army. Parliament ordered that the royal arms should be removed from all paper, especially the large sheets of paper which were used for the Parliamentary Journal. Cromwell ordered that a jester's head should replace the royal arms as a watermark, as a sign of contempt, although this was later dropped. However, the name foolscap stuck even though the watermark was removed and ever since then paper of a large size has been called foolscap.

A third explanation is that "foolscap" comes from the two Italian words, "foglia capa", which mean a first-sized sheet, or a large page.

You can decide for yourself which explanation you like best.

A TRUE STORY

THE PIRATE OF THE RIO GRANDE

It was September, 1836. The Brazilian province of Rio Grande do Sul had rebelled against Pedro 11, the Emperor of Brazil and declared itself to be an independent republic. "The Brazilians," proclaimed Benito Goncalves who had been nominated President, "want to be the masters of their own destiny".

The Imperial troops, however, immediately moved into the attack. On 4th October, the Rio Grande army was routed . . .

. . . But the Republicans refusing to accept defeat, began guerilla warfare . . .

. . . While Goncalves and his secretary, an Italian called Zambeccari, were arrested.

Zambeccari was imprisoned in the fortress of Santa Cruz, at Rio de Janeiro. And there, one morning in the February of 1837 . . .

There's a boat coming in, Sergeant.

It must be bringing the two men who have permission to visit the prisoner.

Your papers, gentlemen !

Here they are. You will find everything in order, Sergeant !

A little later . . . . .

Me ? Does somebody still remember me ?

You've got visitors !

Come in, you two !

Rossetti ! How on earth ?

Keep quiet. We got in on the pretence that we had come from Italy to bring you news of your family.

First, let me introduce you to a friend of mine, Giuseppe Garibaldi.

riends? I
I have friends,
then?

Yes, and they are anxious to fight for the Republic.

But what can I do now?

You could give us a letter giving us permission to act on your behalf and organise a fleet.

With this letter, Rossetti planned to rally the Republican supporters.

We will attack the Imperial forces. We will give them no peace.

With a private fleet, our flag will fly once more.

dy? Thanks for your gentlemen. Are you ning to Italy immediately?

Time's up. Out.

Not mmediately.

We will stay in Rio for a short while. Write to us if you can.

Yes. If I can, I'll send you some letters.

Garibaldi and Rossetti left the fortress of Santa Cruz.

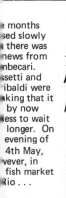

e months sed slowly there was news from nbecari. ssetti and ibaldi were king that it by now less to wait longer. On evening of 4th May, ever, in fish market Rio . . .

Mr. Rossetti?

At your service.

We know that you have a boat.

Yes, we have a boat, the "Mazzini".

Take us on board, please.

Eh, just a moment. . .

Garibaldi, suppose.

But how do you know me? Who are you?

We will discuss that on board, not here.

We have some letters for you . . . from Santa Cruz.

And a little later on board the "Mazzini".

Yes. As from this moment you are soldiers of the Rio Grande Republic.

Zambeccari's Letter!

Some Italians enlisted. Others gave money. Provisions and weapons were put on board the ship . . .

And finally, on the 7th May, 1837 . . .

Let us be off, men! Hoist the mainsail.

The "Mazzini" left. The great adventure of Garibaldi, a privateer of the Rio Grande Republican Forces, was about to begin . . .

A few days later, to the south of Rio.

A sail, Garibaldi!

I... Bra... scho...

Right. Get ready for action, Carniglia.

Ahoy, there! Heave to!

Who hails us? Who are you?

Stop in the name of the Republic of Rio Grande!

What the deuce? They're pirates!

The schooner "Luisa" surrendered.

In the name of the Republic of Rio Grande, I take possession of this ship and her cargo.

I . . . I protest.

Protest as much as you like. Quickly, men, bring everything on board.

Suddenly.

Spare me, Sir, I beg of you.

Stop cringing. Get up, you sniffling coward.

See these diamonds. They are for you. But please spare my life.

Diamonds, eh?

They are yours. Don't kill me.

Keep your diamonds for some other occasion. Your life is in no danger.

ibaldi scuttled the "Mazzini" and hoisted the flag of the Rio Grande on the "Luisa".

I . . . I protest!

We too are protesting, against the Emperor.

Garibaldi christened the schooner "Farropilha", which means "Rabble", a name the Imperial supporters gave to the Republicans . . .

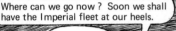

Where can we go now? Soon we shall have the Imperial fleet at our heels.

I think we should head south, towards Uruguay.

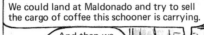

We could land at Maldonado and try to sell the cargo of coffee this schooner is carrying.

And then we could go on to Montevideo . . .

A good idea. We have many friends there.

A few days later the "Farropilha" reached Maldonado.

Here we are. Let's hope we can recruit more volunteers in Montevideo.

Who knows? We may even find another ship. That would be very satisfactory.

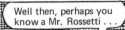

30th May, Rossetti set out on horseback for Montevideo.

I'll be back quickly, my friends.

And with other republicans.

Don't hurry, Rossetti. It's comfortable here at Maldonado.

Rossetti rode on for three days, and stopped for food at an inn at the gates of Montevideo. While he was eating . . .

Are you a foreigner, Sir?

Me? Yes, I'm an Italian.

Italian, eh?

Well then, perhaps you know a Mr. Rossetti . . .

Perhaps I do. Why?

Well, if you see him, tell him not to come to Montevideo. The police are waiting for him there.

The police? Why do they want him?

Who can say ? I think the Governor of Montevideo wants to do a favour for the Emperor of Brazil.

Suddenly the man lowered his voice . . .

Don't lose any time. Escape ! Hide ! The streets are swarming with soldiers.

What about Garibaldi and the others who remained at Maldonado ?

We will think of a way of warning them. We are republicans like you.

Tell him then . . .

. . . to come, when he can, to the Jesus Maria Point. And thanks, friend.

Meanwhile, at sea off Maldonado, a Brazilian warship was standing by. For his part, the Governor of Uruguay was sending two frigates to capture the "Farropilha".

But the messenger sent by Rossetti had warned Garibaldi . . .

He will wait for me at Jesus Maria Point, you say ?

It's all taken care of, sir. Rossetti is safe by now. You must go to him.

Yes. But get going now. There is no time to lose.

Thank you. Tell Rossetti that we'll be seeing him soon.

The "Farropilha" weighed anchor under cover of darkness . . .

Set a course to southwards, Carniglia. And keep near the coast.

Right. That scum won't capture us !

After about twenty days sailing along the rocky coasts of Uruguay . . .

That should be the spot. Wonder if Rossetti is there already ?

Suddenly a cry rang out.

Look over there, Captain. Two frigates.

I can't see anyone on board. I don't like this.

two mysterious frigates came closer, and then . . .

From the biggest of the frigates . . .

Stop in the name of Uruguay.

Soldiers! They are teeming with Soldiers!!

Hard a-starboard. We're going to run for it.

The privateers worked feverishly adjusting the sails.

Faster men. Faster!

But at that moment . . .

Fire!

Aaah!

Fiorentino!

Poor lad!

Look sharp! Be ready for a fight, men.

frigates approached the "Farropilha" oard her.

Fire, men. Fire!

Surrender!

Get back, you louts.

The fight was violent. The soldiers were driven back, but they tried once more to come on board . . .

The helm! There is no-one at the helm.

I'll take the helm. Watch the sides, Carniglia!

Watch out, Giuseppe!

Aagh!

Keep at it, men! We'll wipe out this rabble!

Having been violently repulsed once mor the Uruguayans retreated . . .

They are retreating! Victory! Victory!

They are going!

Victory, but . . .

Giuseppe!

But . . . is he dead?

He's been hit. But, he's not dead, not yet . . .

The "Farropilha" managed to move som distance away from the two frigates. But Garibaldi was terribly injured.

Give me something to bandage him with. And watch the sails.

Courage, Giuseppe. Don't give up.

Where shall we head for now?

The Brazilians will be after us!

We can't stay anywhere along this coast now, Carniglia!

Giuseppe, you are the Captain. Where sh we go? Can you hear me? Show us th course to set.

...nt out the course! Garibaldi's misty eyes ...nned the map, and his finger pointed to a ...t...

...o up here? Up the Parana River?

Set course to the West. We are going up the Parana!

The indomitable "Farropilha", after sailing for several days, began to move up the muddy waters of the Parana River...

...d the body of Giacomo Fiorentino, who died in ...mbat, was entrusted to the gloomy waters of the ...at river!

Poor Giacomo! He did not deserve such a death, nor such a burial.

Carniglia, you must promise me something.

...mise? What must ...omise you, Giuseppe?

If I die, promise me you will bury me on land. Don't throw me into the sea. Carniglia, my friend, like you did Fiorentino.

Don't worry. You've no reason to fear death.

Promise me, I beg of you. Don't throw me into the sea. Swear to it.

...swear to it. If you should die, Giuseppe, ...will dig your grave myself. And you will ...lie in peace. But keep calm now.

At that moment...

A ship!

An Argentinian schooner. Signal to them that we need a doctor urgently.

After several frenzied signals, a reply was received from the Argentinian schooner.

They're answering. There's no doctor aboard. But they're sending us medicines.

Look! They are launching a boat!

A small boat reached the "Farropilha" bringing medicines.

You are going to be all right, Giuseppe

Garibaldi pulled through, yes, and the "Farropilha", sailing up the Parana river, reached the Argentinian port of Gualeguay during the early part of July.

But there, the police were waiting for them, for the ship's route had been observed.

You are under arrest. Your ship is being held by the Government of the Republic of Argentina!

Thus ended Garibaldi's first adventure at se After the schooner had been seized, he was sent to a fever-hospital.

And there, after a few weeks . . .

Look! You have been carrying this bullet around in your body for nearly a month. Thank goodness, it's out.

Doctor, what about my ship?

Now, keep calm. Don't worry about that.

Tell me what has happened to my ship and crew?

Your ship has been seized, sir.

And my friends?

Take this. Your friends are free. They have been sent to Montevideo. You must not worry about them.

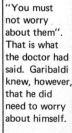

"You must not worry about them". That is what the doctor had said. Garibaldi knew, however, that he did need to worry about himself.

Then, am I in prison

Oh no. But you may not leave the town, that is all. They say that you are a pirate.

122

But I truly believe that you are an honest man. I'll come and see you again shortly.

After a few weeks, Garibaldi recovered from the fever. He now found himself free, providing he stayed in Gualeguay.

But he was not allowed to forget the restrictions.

...ater, when he visited the Governor...

...not keep sentries on duty just for you. ...me your word that you will not escape, ...shall be forced to put you in prison.

I do not know why I am a prisoner, but I give you my promise.

Cooped up in Gualeguay, while my companions are fighting for freedom.

Six months passed slowly. Garibaldi was confined to Gualeguay. But one day he was called to meet Govenor Millan.

You are to be transferred to La Bajada. You leave tomorrow.

To La Bajada? Why?

Never you mind. Do as you are told. You are a prisoner! Remember that!

I promised to stay in Gualeguay. But if they want to transfer me to somewhere else, the promise is no longer valid.

Garibaldi made up his mind. He would try to escape. A trusted friend obtained a horse for him, together with a guide...

...nd he set off by night, during a storm.

At dawn, after a furious gallop through the night.

Stop! Stop! Now!

We are at the river. Why should we stop?

I have a hunch there may be soldiers near the river.

You go and see. I'll wait for you here.

The guide galloped off towards the forest. Garibaldi, who was out of training for long gallops, rested under a tree, before preparing to resume his journey.

For two hours, he waited.

He is not back. How can I go on without him?

I'll have to chance it. I'll find some way of crossing the river.

Halt, don't move.

Keep still, or we fire.

What the blazes?

You promised not to leave Gualeguay, remember?

I remember. And now I know that I was a fool to trust that guide!

Tied to the saddle, Garribaldi was taken back to Gualeguay. The hot sun and swarms of flies added to his discomfort.

In front of the Governor . . .

Well, here you are. Did you think that you could play the fool with me?

How did you get a horse? Who gave you money? Where did you intend to go?

I'll tell you nothing.

Nothing? I'll make you speak, speak, pirate.

Do your worst.

Talk!

Act dumb, would you? Tie him up. I'll teach the pirate a lesson.

In the dungeons . . .

It is futile. There's nothing I can tell you.

We will see about that. String him up.

124